MW00889448

Was that a
COINCIDENCE
or What!

Signposts from a Friendly Universe

---

*Blessings to
Gordon,
David Crippen*

David Wells Crippen
M.Div., Ph.D.

SUNNIHILL

Copies of *Was That a Coincidence or WHAT!* are available from
www.Amazon.com.

If you like this book, please help spread the word by going to
Amazon.com and writing your review of it.

"David and Karen Crippen have quietly touched the lives of thousands of people around the world (including me). In this immensely entertaining and insightful book, David reveals the pivotal role that synchronicity has played in their lives. Without insisting upon a specifically Christian interpretation of synchronicity, David moves all readers to ponder the force in the universe which seems to guide us through life at critical times. People of faith will recognize a Divine Mystery at work here and, hopefully, reflect upon their own encounters with this Holy Mystery."

RADM (Retired) D. E. Snider, MD, MPH
Chief Science Officer, Centers for Disease Control and Prevention
Atlanta, Georgia

"The Reverend Dr. David Crippen has written of life's holy synchronicities and of the presence of God in the everyday cycle of living. The message is an important one—that Almighty God chooses to be God-With-Us. Indeed, the Incarnation is fundamental to Christian theology, for it offers us both hope and promise. In this book, Father Crippen has shared some of his story in a way that testifies to the intersection of human with the divine. I am happy to commend his story to others, for I believe that we may all identify parts of our experience that we share and have in common with his."

The Right Reverend Charles vonRosenberg
Retired Bishop of the Episcopal Diocese of East Tennessee
Charleston, South Carolina

"David Crippen has written a compelling book that is evocative, whimsical, and engaging. It triggers a response from all senses and takes us to places of remembering events and people along life's journey. Crippen offers us an opportunity to be filled with 'encounters of a spirit kind,' causing a rethinking of everyday life and asking, 'Was that really just a coincidence?'"

The Reverend Doctor Juanita E. Leonard
Professor of Christian Mission Emerita
Anderson University School of Theology
Anderson, Indiana

"I got a wonderful feeling of comfort in reading your Conclusion. I truly believe what you are conveying here--that we are living in this universe of loving energy that is always conspiring for our ultimate good. I think many others who read this book will feel comforted also, and it will be an encouragement to them."

Tabitha Bilbrey
Licensed Massage Therapist
Chattanooga, Tennessee

for Karen, dearest partner, adventurer and spiritual seeker; lover and soul mate; and fellow traveler on this incredibly exciting ride we're on called Life.

for Bekki, Debbi, and Tabbi, our three amazing, grace-filled daughters, who accompanied us on all our journeys, and whose spiritual insights far exceed mine, together with

the host of fur-faced, feathered, and finned creatures that have filled our home over the years,

all of whom have taught me that God is everywhere.

CONTENTS

v

"The most important question a person can ask is, 'Is the universe a friendly place?'"

—Albert Einstein

INTRODUCTION

I never paid much attention to coincidences, that is, until one day there was the "coincidence" that changed my life forever. Hello, Karen!

That was the day I walked into the five-and-dime store where she worked and was so struck with the sight of her, that even though she was going with another boy, I felt we had a future together.

I waited two weeks to call her and bingo! They had broken up and I moved into the number one position.

It was 1959 and I was a student at Florida Southern College in Lakeland. My Old Testament History professor had suggested, on more than one occasion, that the Israelites must have considered the number *forty* to be a sacred number. No wonder, because they had wandered in the wilderness for *forty* years, it rained on Noah for *forty* days and *forty* nights, and Kings David and Solomon each reigned over Israel for *forty* years. Even in the New Testament, the writer relates that Jesus was tempted in the wilderness for *forty* days.

After dating each other for several weeks, our romance began to blossom. Then one day I realized that our combined ages, when we met, was approximately *forty* years. I didn't give it much thought at first, but then one evening several weeks later I decided to crunch the numbers and figure out exactly how close to forty years it was, when we first met.

Calculating the number of days beyond our 39 years of combined ages, I added the number of days in each month from Karen's birthday, May 1, to the day we met; then added them to the number of days from my birthday, May 13, to the day we met. I found that on the day we met, November 6, we had lived apart for exactly 39 years and 365 days! Wow! With that phenomenal discovery, I was convinced something pretty major was going on, so I asked her to marry me.

That was the beginning of a lifetime of meaningful coincidences, many of them so significant that I began to believe there must be an *unseen power* at work.

Researching the matter, I discovered I wasn't alone. Carl Jung, distinguished Swiss psychiatrist and founder of analytical psychiatry, who, himself experienced meaningful coincidences, coined the term "synchronicity" to describe "simultaneous occurrences that are meaningfully related." Synchronicities, in Jung's thinking, would include occurrences that lead us to a broader, more illumined awareness, and sometimes toward our deepest calling. Many people I've talked with believe that coincidences, especially life-guiding coincidences, are God-inspired.

From all the synchronicities that have radically re-directed my life, to those that have simply put a grin on my face, I have come to believe that we have not been left here alone on this planet just to fend for ourselves, but that there is, indeed, a powerful life force in the world and in our lives constantly at work for our our ultimate good.

CHAPTER 1

MEADOWLARK

Tampa, Florida 1963

"Wake at dawn with a winged heart and give thanks for another day of loving."

—Kahlil Gibran

Young couples in love often like to play silly little games together. Karen and I had been married nearly two years and were still playing a little game we had invented shortly after we were married. We didn't have a name for our game and neither of us ever asked the other if she or he wanted to play. The game went like this: the first one to wake up in the morning woke the other and said something like, "Good morning, Ms. Butterfly." When I would say that, she would blink her eyes, yawn, and say something like, "Good morning, Mr. Aardvark." And then she would laugh. But that was just the beginning of the game. From then on throughout the day, she was Ms. Butterfly and I was Mr. Aardvark. Aardvark just happened to be my least favorite name. I never should have told Karen that, because whenever she couldn't think of another kind of animal, I always ended up being Mr. Aardvark.

One day something happened, related to our game, which gave us pause. The "occurrence" in question happened during my first year of teaching. I had what I thought was an exceptional class of fifth-grade kids. One little boy, Wayne King, was readily noticeable in a number of ways. Wayne always managed to be "Number One" in not getting his homework in on time. He also had a penchant for flirting with and teasing the girls. Interestingly, even though Wayne was the shortest boy in the class, he nonetheless was a scrappy little guy and relished playing the role of class clown.

One day when Karen had the afternoon off, she came to my classroom and sat in the back, just to observe. At the conclusion of school that day, she told me Wayne had turned around in his seat, smiled, and then winked at her several times.

Near the end of the school year I was awakened early one morning by the sleepy voice of Karen saying, "Good morning, Mr. Meadowlark." A smile must have spread across my face, because I liked the sound of the name, Meadowlark. It had a nice ring to it. I had no idea what a meadowlark looked like, but I knew it was a bird. Nevertheless, I was happy to know I would be Mr. Meadowlark all that day.

Later that morning, my class was lined up outside, single file, getting ready to walk to the lunchroom. It was a beautiful Florida spring morning and the fragrance of freshly mown grass permeated the air. Suddenly, much to the amazement of the entire class, a large smartly dressed bird with feathers of yellow, black, and white swooped down out of the sky and landed in the grass just a few feet from us. Without missing a beat, a loud crystal clear voice from the back of the line called out, rising above all the other children's chattering, "LOOK! There's a meadowlark! I love meadowlarks!"

It was Wayne.

How did he know it was a meadowlark, especially when I, his teacher, didn't even know that? And how was it that that particular bird, a meadowlark, paid us a visit that particular morning? There was no way little Wayne could have known I was "Mr. Meadowlark" that day; and

2

if he did, I don't believe he would have hollered out what he did. To say I was stunned would be putting it mildly; so much so, that I cannot recall anything else that happened that day, except for sharing the incident with Karen, who was as astonished as I was.

We puzzled over how the entire event could have been coordinated so perfectly: I mean, that a meadowlark, of all birds, could have flown down and landed so very close, at that precise moment in time, when we were all outside, and that of all my students, little Wayne shouted out what he did...given what Karen named me that very morning.

We were convinced this had to be more than just an "ordinary coincidence." The thing that puzzled us just as much as the timing of the incident and the fact that the bird was identified by one of my least studious pupils, was how the word "love" was injected into the event. It seemed to us as though Wayne's calling out the word "love" had somehow elevated the moment to a higher reality.

Pondering all that had happened from the moment we awakened, to the shouting out of "I love meadowlarks," we knew that, somehow, it was all connected. But how?

And, oh yes, I checked out a bird book shortly after the incident. Sure enough, the bird we saw was, in fact, a meadowlark.

CHAPTER 2

CROSSROADS

Tampa 1965

"If I'd gotten the job I wanted at Montgomery Ward, I suppose I would never have left Illinois."

—Ronald Reagan

Did you ever dream of something you really wanted to do, then just before fully realizing that dream, watch helplessly as it fell apart? Only later did you see that all which transpired did so for the best.

I was a student at the University of South Florida, working on a master's degree with a dream of one day teaching educational psychology in college. Dr. Donald Lantz, my academic advisor, suggested that I apply for the Ph.D. program in educational psychology at the University of Minnesota, which he considered had the best program in that field, and where he felt certain I would be accepted. Taking his advice, I applied only to Minnesota with hopes of receiving an acceptance letter sometime in late winter or early spring.

February came, and every day I approached my mail box with hopes of receiving a letter of acceptance. In mid-March, I found a postcard in my box from the Peace Corps in Washington. It read, "You are invited to train for a Community Development project in Hilo, Hawaii, starting June 11 for later deployment to Malaysia." WOW! That was a dream Karen and I had given up on months before. Nearly two years earlier, we had made a trip to the Peace Corps office in Washington to discuss the various possibilities that Peace Corps had to offer. We had been excited over the possibility of serving our country and fellow man in this way, so we'd applied. But, two years had passed, and our hopes were now pinned on my working toward earning the Ph.D. Having heard nothing from the Peace Corps since we'd applied, we simply had given up and forgotten about it. Certainly, the invitation to join the Peace Corps excited us; but at the end of the day, we decided that it would be best for me to go for the Ph.D.

The next day I picked up the mail as usual, and to my delight, there was the long-awaited letter from the University of Minnesota. Shaking with excitement, I tore into the envelope. As I read through the letter, my heart sank: "...we regret to inform you that your application for admission to the Ph.D. program in educational psychology has been denied."

How could this be? I called Dr. Lantz and explained the situation. After listening to my story, he invited both Karen and me to meet him at his home the following evening. There, he and his wife, Marilyn, talked with us about options we might want to consider.

Finally he said, "One of the things Marilyn and I have done in past years when facing tough decisions, was to think in terms of doors closing and doors opening. While it's disappointing that the door you hoped to walk through is now closed, here's another door that has just opened."

We discussed the timing of the responses we had received: the rejection from Minnesota and the invitation to Peace Corps training. We talked about the fact that, if we had gone ahead with a Ph.D. program then, we probably would never have experienced what had been our first love, the Peace Corps. And if the Peace Corps invitation had come when we had hoped it would, I would probably *not* be completing a master's degree. But because of the *precise timing* of the events that transpired, I was not only able to complete my master's degree, and attend Peace Corps training, but also earn the Ph.D.

CHAPTER 3

SURPRISE MEETING

Los Angeles 1965

*"...the universe is filled with all sorts of fortuitous encounters,
intuitions, and mysterious coincidences, all pointing to a higher
purpose behind our lives, and in fact, behind all of human
history."*

—James Redfield

Like many young Americans who grew up middle-class in the 40's and 50's, we were taught to seek divine guidance when facing important life decisions. But then, sometimes guidance comes before you even ask for it.

It was already hot, as we arrived at the Tampa International Airport, with tickets to our ultimate destination—Kuala Lumpur, Malaysia—tucked away in our suitcase. Smiles and tears filled the faces of our family and friends who were there to say their good-byes. The feeling of butterflies took over my stomach, as we showed our boarding passes to the airline representatives at the gate, then climbed on board and settled into our seats.

Karen clenched my hand as we lifted off. I had the feeling we were somehow leaving an "old" life behind, and that a new life lay before us, a life that held mystery and adventure. We circled the city of Tampa below us and

9

headed west. Peering out the window through the scattered clouds, we bade farewell to the Florida that had been our home for most of our lives. As the plane leveled off, we began to talk about what we might do in Los Angeles that evening during our overnight layover, before proceeding to San Francisco the next morning. "Let's go to Hollywood while we're in L. A. We might as well. It's not that far from the airport. Who knows, we might even see a movie star," I quipped. "Yeah," Karen pitched in, "we can catch a bus from the airport into Hollywood and find a hotel there, and then go to a nice restaurant."

Upon arriving in L. A., we picked up our luggage from baggage claim and headed out of the terminal to catch a bus into Hollywood. Looking around, we could see what a "mega" airport we were in:each airline had its own terminal. We sat down on our bags several feet back from the curb, waiting for a city bus to arrive, and watched as an inter-terminal tram pulled up and stopped directly in front of us. The tram was a smallish, open-air vehicle that had bench seats facing each other. One lone passenger was on board, a gentleman with sunglasses who happened to be facing us. There were no other people around waiting for the tram, so apparently the driver thought we were there wanting to board. Suddenly, I noticed that the gentleman on board looked distinctly familiar. I jumped to my feet and ran onto the tram, and to my utter surprise, was greeted with a friendly, "Why, David Crippen! What are you doing here?" Just then, the driver began to pull away, leaving my panic-stricken wife back at the curb with our bags. Realizing we were moving, I called to the driver to stop and wait, while I got Karen and our bags on board. The gentleman was, indeed, who I thought it might be, Dr. Robert Reardon, who had been my pastor at a Brookhaven, Pennsylvania church when I was just a boy. He later became the president of Anderson University in Indiana, where I attended my freshman year. We had not seen each other for several years.

Recovering from the surprise of our meeting, I told

him Karen and I were on our way to Peace Corps training. He responded, "Dean Newberry, from our School of Theology, and I are on the first leg of a trip around the world; but right now, I'm on my way over to another terminal to see my daughter, Becky, off to Peace Corps training in the Philippines! Why don't you join us for a cup of coffee?"

"Absolutely," I said. "We'd love it."

I remembered that Becky had been born twenty-one years earlier, while Reardon was my pastor, and I was eager to meet the young woman who, like us, was now joining the Peace Corps.

After introductions, we sat down and ordered coffee, and the three of us younger ones talked about what we might expect on our assignments. The conversation then turned to reminiscing. Reardon smiled, as I reminded him of the time we went to a father and son banquet at the YMCA. He laughed when I told him how upset my older brother, John, was when I went as his son, and John had to go as "just our dad's son."

Responding to an urge to move on, I thanked Reardon and made some excuse for having to go. Standing up and grabbing our bags, I said, "We need to go find a city bus stop, instead of a tram stop this time."

Reardon smiled. Then, turning serious, he looked at me and said, "David, Dean Newberry is over at the National Terminal waiting for me, but I want you and Karen to go over there to talk with him before you leave the airport." Reading the fallen expression on my face, he persisted. In a remotely familiar, fatherly tone, he said, "Now, David, I want you and Karen to go speak with him before you leave the airport. He's sitting in the waiting room at the National Airlines terminal. Just get on a tram and run over there." With that, he pulled a small wad of bills from his pocket and stuffed it into my shirt pocket, with the words, "Have a good time tonight."

Walking into the National terminal, I said to Karen, "What in the world are we supposed to say to this guy?

We don't know him and he doesn't know us from Adam." In the waiting room, we immediately spotted a dark haired, dignified-looking gentleman sitting by himself, reading. We walked over to him, "Dean Newberry?"

He looked up from his book. "Yes?"

We introduced ourselves and I explained our surprise meeting with Reardon. "He suggested we come over here and talk with you," I concluded. A faint smile spread across the dean's face as I said this.

We talked for several minutes, then after a quick glance at my watch, I said, "It's been great talking with you, Dean Newberry, but I think we'd better get going and try to find a hotel where we can spend the night."

His smile turned solemn. "David, I have a question. Have you ever considered full-time church service?" I paused, struggling to find an answer that didn't sound rude. Finally, I said something that no doubt left the distinct impression I never had really considered that option. Little did I know, then, the significance of the dean's question, a question that, at the time, was suggesting something that was furthest from my mind, but, at the same time, got buried in my soul as *a seed well planted*.

On the bus into Hollywood, Karen and I talked about the tail-end of our unlikely meeting with Reardon. "Why on Earth did he insist we talk with the dean?" I asked.

"Yeah, it was like he was not going to let us go until we agreed to go meet him."

With that quizzical thought in mind, we both quietly stared out the window at the traffic and unique sights and people on the streets of Hollywood. We had no idea, at that moment, how serendipitous that chance meeting might prove to be.

CHAPTER 4

THE SILENT VOICE

Waikiuka, Hawaii 1965

"Silence is God's first language; everything else is a poor translation."

—Thomas Keating

As we lifted off from L.A. airport northward toward San Francisco, it began to dawn on me that our big dream of months past—which, for a time, had been eclipsed by my infatuation with the hope of getting into a Ph.D. program—was actually beginning to materialize. I settled back and gazed out the window at the great expanse of downy white clouds drifting leisurely below, and my heart told me *this* was where we were supposed to be.

When we arrived at the designated waiting area in the San Francisco airport, several other Peace Corps trainees had already gathered, waiting for the charter flight that would take us to Honolulu. They all appeared to be in their early and mid-twenties, and, like us, excited and a little nervous. We had been told by our liaison we would board for Honolulu that night, and then, in the morning, take a shuttle flight to Hilo.

High over the Pacific, I peered out the window into the pitch black night sky. A feeling of awe washed over me, of the immensity of what lay hidden before us. As the night dragged on, I was too excited to sleep, my mind perpetually wondering about the new adventures awaiting Karen and me.

The eastern sky was just beginning to show the first glimmers of light when we landed at the Honolulu airport. There, we were immediately herded over to a smaller prop-driven plane, and soon were airborne heading toward Hilo on the big island. Out the window, peering eastward, I could see the early morning sun rays piercing the mass of rising mists and clouds over the water. I pondered the Psalm Karen and I had shared with each other before leaving: "If I take the wings of the morning, and dwell in the uttermost parts of the sea, even there your hand will lead me, and your right hand hold me fast." Once again I felt reassured of our decision to be with the Peace Corps.

A blast of warm, humid air hit us in the face, as we disembarked at the Hilo airport. Body weary and a little dazed, we picked up our bags and piled them into a waiting bus. Little did we know this bus had likely been around since World War II, its shock absorbers doing more "shocking" than "absorbing." Grinning and bearing it, we bumped our way up a narrow, winding road that took us gradually up the eastern slope of Mauna Kea, the mountain that only recently was declared by National Geographic, to be the world's tallest mountain, when measured from it's base at the bottom of the Pacific Ocean. Karen and I were amazed at the fields of gorgeous purple, white, and yellow orchids that were growing wild out the window. Finally, the bus slowed and turned into a compound where there were several weather worn, wooden frame buildings. We learned later that it had been a rural village school years before.

When the bus came to an abrupt stop, one of the leaders called out to the married couples for us to grab our bags and follow him. Eighteen bedraggled young people trudged along behind the leader, until he stopped us at the front of one of the old frame buildings. If it had ever held a coat of paint, it was many years past.

"This will be your sleeping quarters," he announced, and then promptly turned and left. One of the wives opened the screen door and walked in. Single file, we all followed. Inside, the 14 by 48-foot room was bare, except for nine pairs of cots, each pair an arm's length from the next pair. There were no partitions and no bathroom. It began to dawn on us we had just been given our first assignment in "community development."

After a few moments of stunned silence, one of the husbands said, "We need to get hold of a large roll of wire, some hammers and nails..."

"And some shower curtains to partition off each pair of cots," his wife chimed in.

Early the next morning, we were awakened by someone shouting outside the front door in a language Karen and I didn't understand. A while later, after a hearty breakfast, we were told to report to our classroom in thirty minutes. The classroom was large and bare, except for 63 desks and chairs, a lectern at the front, and the traditional blackboard. The chatter stopped suddenly when a young Malaysian woman entered the classroom, walked to front and center, and in a clear, crisp voice said, "*Selamat pagi.*" She then motioned with her hands and arms for us to repeat after her. Again and again, she said, "*Selamat pagi,*" with us repeating the phrase over and over, continuously, for at least two minutes. Finally she stopped. Then, glancing around the room at each of us, she smiled and said quietly, "Good morning. This is 'Good morning.'" By the end of the day, we were all greeting each other, asking each other what we wanted to buy, and where was the bathroom, all in Malay.

Training was rigorous, day and night, mostly language, cultural do's and don'ts, and group dynamics. One evening after dinner, we were released for the evening to do as we pleased. We had been hitting it hard for over a month and were ready for a little break; so Karen and I jumped at the opportunity to get away by ourselves. We decided to take a walk up a nearby mountain path. It was a gradual climb upward, where we saw small trees, bushes and lava rock formations, but no houses, buildings or any signs of human life.

We continued walking as we watched the sun disappear behind the mountain. The sky took on hues of pale yellow and pink. We slowed our walk as the twilight faded and the night set in. Suddenly, we realized it was so dark, we could hardly see our hands in front of our faces. In the distance, we saw the glow from the city of Hilo, and tiny specks of flickering light from slow-moving vehicles and houses scattered along the coast. Further out was the faint light of a passing ship.

It was a moonless night. We stopped and stood motionless, not speaking. There was a deep silence, not a sound, not even a breeze. I sensed a profound tranquility, like the whole earth had stopped moving. Suddenly, in the stillness, I was gripped by an overwhelming feeling that we were witnessing something powerful.

Awestruck, I whispered to Karen that I thought I felt God's Presence. She agreed—she felt it too. We wondered aloud, whether there was a message we should be divining from this Presence. Nothing clear, at that moment, emerged for either of us. We agreed that there must be a message, but we were just not getting it; so we decided to repeat the words of a chorus we had learned in our youth group back home: "Speak, my Lord, speak my Lord, and I'll be quick to answer."

Still in a state of wonderment, we began our slow descent down the mountain.

CHAPTER 5

INSPIRED MOMENT

Hilo, Hawaii 1965

*"Coincidences are homing beacons. They are secret handshakes
from the universe. They are extraordinary sources of guidance
and direction."*

—Robert Moss

The days flew by, as we dreamed and talked about
the details of our coming assignment to live and work
with the river people in North Borneo. Excitement hardly
describes how Karen and I felt.

One day, we awoke with pancakes and sausage being
the order of the morning. These had obviously been
prepared with just the right amount of everything I like in
a pancake—they were delicious—but Karen's and my
progress with the now-mandated chopsticks was
frustratingly slow. We watched with open admiration as
Fousie, our favorite Malaysian language instructor, neatly
and efficiently folded each little pancake into quarters
and placed it in his mouth, while still managing to
maintain a running stream of conversation with his
students. Karen and I decided we just might starve to
death before this training was over.

Most of the other trainees had finished their
breakfast and moved out of the dining hall, when Karen

leaned over and whispered in my ear, "You know, I'm a week late for my period."

I pulled back and looked at her, "You've never been late before. Why didn't you tell me?"

"We couldn't do anything about it, and, well, I didn't want to worry you."

"Worry! You know, if you're pregnant, we'll be sent home, just like Carol and Tom when they found out she was pregnant."

"Keep your voice down," Karen said, cupping her hand to her mouth. "It's probably just due to all the changes we're going through."

"Yeah, but you're always right on time every month, right to the day."

"Well, there's nothing we can do."

"Right, so let's just drop it for now. We'll talk about it later. Come on, it's almost time for class."

Another week passed and we were just finishing supper, while most of the other trainees had already cleared out. Karen had been quiet throughout most of the meal, when suddenly our eyes met and locked. After a few moments, I said, "I know what you're thinking."

"I just can't believe this is happening," she said, as she began to tear up. I reached across the table and took her hand.

We had avoided talking about what we might do if she were pregnant. "I just don't want to even think about it now," I said.

"But we're going to have t..." Her voice trailed off as Jim, who entertained us evenings with his guitar and charming voice, entered the dining hall and headed toward us.

"What are we singing tonight, Jim?" I asked, forcing a smile.

"All our favorites!" he said, flashing his huge grin. Jim and his wife, Nancy, helped us all maintain our sanity with their music, singing all the popular folk songs of the 60's like "Yellow Bird," "This Land is Your Land," and "If I Had a Hammer."

Jim had a unique way of getting everybody singing and laughing for about thirty minutes after supper. He did this nearly every evening, before our last class of the day.

After the first song, Karen turned to me and whispered, "I'm really going to miss this, if we have to go."

"Come on, let's sing," I whispered back. "Just forget that for now...and then on Saturday, after lunch, when we have some time, we'll get our heads together and talk about it."

"Saturday...okay, we'll talk about it Saturday."

When Saturday morning arrived, I woke up with a start. Karen was already awake, lying on her back staring at the ceiling. "How do you feel?" I ventured.

"Just the same." Her sullen response matched the sadness in her eyes.

"Well, I guess this is the day."

"I've got an idea," she said. "After lunch, let's head down to Hilo Bay, just the two of us, and find a place where we can clear out our heads."

"Great idea."

There was little traffic on the narrow winding road that led down to town. We had learned, from experience, that by simply sticking out our thumbs when a car came, we could usually get a free ride, if there was any room at all in the car. Sometimes, it meant packing us in like sardines; but we quickly got used to that kind of temporary "close quarters."

The first car to come by picked us up and took us to a

spot within walking distance of the bay. We walked until we found a deserted place, accented by a huge boulder that overlooked the vast expanse before us. Climbing up onto it, we looked out over the water, into what seemed like a living blue plane of infinity. To our left, along the curved shoreline, were the city docks, behind which were shops and stores. Straight out and to our right was the bay that "somewhere out there" joined the Pacific Ocean.

After absorbing the beauty of the environment and making small talk, the inevitable moment came when we knew we had to deal with what we were going to do. I verbalized a little prayer, expressing our hope for insight into what we should do and where we should go.

We began talking about possibilities:staying in Hawaii and trying to find work , going back to Florida, settling in another part of the States. We knew from our training, so far, that we both loved learning about other cultures. Finally, when we felt we had exhausted every conceivable alternative, we fell silent, and just sat, looking out at the sea.

Suddenly, Karen blurted out, "Why don't we become missionaries!"

"YES! Of course!" was my instantaneous response.

Out of the blue, it seemed we had the answer.

"I don't know why we didn't think about this before," Karen said, "because you know, there are several people in my family who were missionaries."

"Yeah, and besides that," I added, "if we can't go to a developing country to help people through the auspices of the government, then why not go through the church?"

"Yeah...and besides making sense, it just feels right!"

Up to that time, I had been looking out at the sea. But then I turned, and looked at Karen. "Yeah, it just feels right."

From that moment on, we talked about nothing else. After just a few minutes in a flurry of excited chatter, it appeared our search had ended and our fate was sealed. Having had no experience applying for missionary training, or what the training itself might consist of, or what we might do as missionaries, our zealous conversation perhaps could have been compared to two small children talking about becoming deep-sea divers or astronauts.

Recalling our experience on the mountain some weeks before, Karen said, "Remember what happened on the mountain, and our prayer, "Speak my Lord...and I'll be quick to answer?"

We stayed on the boulder, talking about all the exotic places we might go and what we might do, until we noticed the sky in the west turning yellow and pink.

"I have a suggestion," I said. "The fact that this idea of becoming missionaries came up so fast and we've had only a matter of minutes to even think about it, I suggest we go back and sleep on it. Then, we can make a final decision tomorrow."

"Yeah!" Karen answered, with a buoyant lilt in her voice.

I jumped off the boulder and raised my arms, signaling her to jump. She flew into my arms, inadvertently knocking me down, and we rolled around and around on the ground together laughing.

CHAPTER 6

SILENCE IS BROKEN

Hilo, Hawaii 1965

"Rather than a self-chosen path, we are asked to allow it to be Spirit-chosen and guided."

—Diane Harmony

A stream of early morning sunlight pouring through the open shuttered window announced the dawn of a new day. It was Sunday morning, the only day we could sleep in. The shower-curtain partitions dividing up our group's sleeping quarters had given way to the sultry, tropical heat, and a glance down the two rows of cots suggested everyone was still asleep and I was the only one awake. My thoughts turned to our experience on the boulder overlooking the bay the day before, and I felt the flutter of a butterfly in my stomach. Soon, though, squeaking cots and scattered whisperings announced the start-up of the day.

"Let's go sailing!" we heard someone say.

"Yeah! What a beautiful day for sailing!"

Karen and I had already begun to dress for church; but then, sailing on the bay sounded like a great option, especially since we were beginning to realize this *could*, very well, be our last Sunday there.

"On the other hand," I said, "if today is our day to make a decision, maybe we ought go to church."

We had discovered the little church about two miles down the road toward town, and attended several times on the Sundays when we weren't sleeping in. We had never seen any other Caucasians there, except the pastor and his wife and two children, plus an elderly couple. The music minister was a heavyset Hawaiian man and the organist was a blind Japanese man. The rest of the congregation was made up mostly of Hawaiians, Japanese, and Filipinos.

At sermon time, the pastor introduced a guest preacher, the Rev. William Fisher, a well-known evangelist in the Nazarene Church, who was on a world tour. Just before the final hymn, Rev. Fisher invited anyone who had special prayer needs or requests to come forward and kneel at the altar rail. As people began going forward, I whispered to Karen, "Don't we have something special to pray about?" We went forward.

Immediately following the dismissal, while we were still at the front, Rev. Fisher came straight over to us and asked, "What are you doing here?"

"We're training with the Peace Corps," I answered proudly.

His response was not at all what I expected. Standing just inches away, he pointed his finger straight into my chest. "What you are doing is SECOND BEST!" he said emphatically. I was shocked and humiliated at his words and his gesture, which I felt were rude. Without even acknowledging his response, I turned to Karen and said, "Let's go."

As we approached the door to go out, I noticed a tall, white gentleman in a black suit, whom we had never seen before, standing between us and the door. We started to go around him, but he stepped in front of us, blocking our way. He then leaned down to where he was right in our faces, and questioned us, "What are you doing here?"

24

I thought to myself, "What is going on here?" But then, to answer his question, I said, "We are training with the Peace Corps."

His voice was gentle, but direct, "Can you preach about *Jesus* in the Peace Corps?"

"I'm not a preacher, I'm a teacher," I answered.

In the same kindly tone he asked, "Can you *teach* about Jesus in the Peace Corps?"

"As a teacher," I said, "I don't mention the name Jesus, but I do try to model my life after his."

"I know, I know," he said, maintaining his gentle tone, "but can you *actually teach about him?*"

Not wanting to give in, but feeling trapped, I simply answered, "No."

Without a word, he turned and was gone.

Just then, the elderly Caucasian lady called to us, "Would you like a ride back up to camp?"

"Yes, thank you. By the way, who was that tall, white man in the black suit?"

"I never saw him before. Unusual to get visitors up here, but perhaps he's someone from town."

We got into the back seat of their car and remained quiet, reeling from our last two encounters.

At lunch, most of the other trainees were out. We ate in relative silence throughout the meal, sharing little smiles, savoring our secret, actually *two* secrets, and wondering what the future might hold.

As we cleared our trays, I said, "Let's go find a quiet place out back where we can talk. We need to make a firm decision about what we're going to do."

We made our way out the screen door in the back of the dining hall and walked until we found a secluded spot, a place where the ground was covered with the incredibly colorful miniature orchids from which the

25

beautiful Hawaiian leis are made. We sat down on the ground and I took a deep breath. Down at the core of my being, I had the feeling we were nearing the end of another chapter in our lives and were about to enter the next.

I looked at Karen and said, "I was thinking, I don't want us to look back on our experience here and have to say that *why* we became missionaries, if we do, was because you became pregnant. If we become missionaries, I think we need to decide that we would have done it whether you were *pregnant or not*."

"Yes, I agree," Karen said.

"We have to be sure about this, then."

I breathed a short prayer, then looked over at Karen. "How do you feel?"

Her response was simple, but sure. "*Yes.*"

"*Me, too,*" I echoed.

Feeling confident that our decision was clear, we spent the rest of the afternoon working on a letter to the missionary board of our church, introducing ourselves, and inquiring about the possibility of beginning training.

By late afternoon the letter was done, and with both signatures at the bottom we sealed the envelope.

CHAPTER 7

TIMING

In Flight – Nashville, Tennessee 1965-67

"...the whole universe, despite its immensity and solidity, is a projection of God's nature. Those astonishing events we call miracles give us clues to the workings of this ineffable intelligence."

—Deepak Chopra

Bags in hand, Karen and I walked across the tarmac and up the ramp into the waiting plane. As she slipped into a window seat, I struggled with our bags, trying to make them fit into the small, overhead compartment. When I finally took my seat, Karen was silent, as she peered out the window. Full of mixed feelings myself, I asked her, "How do you feel?"

"I can't believe this is happening," she answered sullenly. "I don't know whether to laugh or cry."

I reached over and took hold of her hand, as the engines roared, signaling we were about to begin moving. Moments later, we were speeding down the runway. I squeezed her hand as we lifted off. Our heads were still spinning from the turnarounds in our lives over the past two weeks. Our dream to become missionaries had suddenly become a real possibility, when we got word that we had been accepted for missionary training, although we weren't guaranteed that we would actually end up on a foreign field. One comforting thought was, wherever we *did* end up, we'd be together; and not just the two of us, but three.

Minutes later, we were looking down on billowy, white clouds against a background of vast, blue ocean. Karen finally broke the silence, "I have to go to the bathroom." I stood and let her pass, then watched as she made her way to the rear of the plane. I sat back down, pulled an airlines magazine out of the pocket in front of me, and began paging through it thoughtlessly.

When Karen came back, I stood as she squeezed by to her seat and sat down. I glanced over and noticed she was crying. Looking dazed, she was silent for a moment, then blurted out, "I'm not pregnant!"

"What do you mean? Of course you are!"

Choking the words out in a muffled tone, "I'm BLEEDING! I'm NOT pregnant."

I was speechless. She laid her head on my chest and broke into muted sobs.

"How can this be?" I asked. "Can we go back?"

"No," she said, lifting up her tear-stained face. Looking at me, she added, "For one thing, I don't know what's going on in my body. This has never happened to me before, and I don't know what it means."

Yeah, we need to get you to a doctor."

We sat in confused silence, listening to the engines purring us away from our long-dreamed-of destination, toward a yet-to-be-revealed future.

Wiping her face with the back of her hand, she looked at me, hesitated, then, in a halting voice, said, "The *timing* of this whole thing has just been too perfect."

Thoughtlessly, I replied, "You know, I was just starting to look forward to having a baby."

She began weeping again. "This doesn't mean we

have to give up having a baby!" she said between sobs. "Just for *now*, we have to give it up. *Timing*! Think of the *timing* of what's been happening to us!"

"Okay. But it just seems like we always get our hopes up for things, and then something happens such that it doesn't turn out."

Karen clasped my hand, as the plane slowly began its descent. Gazing out the window, I could see the famous Honolulu shoreline coming into view. *Timing*, I thought, *timing*.

At the end of our first year of training, we were told we would be going to Kenya, and throughout that year, we had hung onto the vision of going as a family of three; but so far, things were not looking very hopeful. By the start of our second and final year, we had become increasingly discouraged over the prospects of having a baby of our own; so we began inquiring into the possibility of adoption. Then, one day we received a phone call from the father of a close young lady friend, whom Karen and I had not seen for two or three years. He explained that his daughter was pregnant, and because she was not married, she did not want to raise the child by herself. He said, "She is looking for a couple who would give her child a good home." I went weak and nearly dropped the phone.

"Karen," I hollered, "come to the phone!"

We both pressed our ears to the phone in disbelief, as the father of our friend told us about his daughter's desire to give up her baby; and that we were her first choice for receiving the baby, as soon as she or he was born. When we finally hung up, we were hysterical with mixed tears of joy and laughter. We immediately began planning for the baby and thinking of possible names. Now, we would go to Kenya as a "real" family, after all.

Then, one December evening, the phone rang. "I'll get it," I said.

"David?"

"Yes, this is David."

The voice was solemn. It was the father of the young mother-to-be. "I'm awfully sorry to have to tell you this, but, as you know, the baby is due soon; and after long and agonizing discussions, we've decided it would be better for her and the baby if the baby were to go to a couple who are not friends of the family, but to a family who we do not know. That way, she believes, it would be easier for her to just leave this whole ordeal behind."

Suddenly, our world of hopes and aspirations collapsed, and our dream of taking this blessed little one with us to Africa utterly dissolved. Stunned, I hung up the phone and, holding onto each other, we wept. "Now, we'll have to go it alone," I sobbed.

January came and a beautiful white blanket of snow covered the ground. One of our professors, Carrie Lou Goddard, with whom we had become good friends, invited us to house-sit her attractive, white brick home while she was on a world tour. One evening after we had moved in, and shortly before her departure, I arrived home late from the library to find Karen dressed in a long, flowing white bathrobe with tiny pink rosebuds. A log fire was burning in the fireplace, and Karen invited me to set my briefcase down and sit in a chair she had placed facing a large tripod with a pad of newsprint set on it. Carrie Lou was already there seated in a comfortable chair. Karen then picked up a marker and slowly began drawing a figure of something on the newsprint; I could not make out what it was. Simultaneously, she began reciting a fable from a book we were reading in preparation for our departure for Kenya, Out of Africa by Isak Dinessan. The fable was about a man who tries and fails at a task, gets up, and tries again and again. Then, finally, in the end, he sees the result of all his steadfast faithfulness, and is rewarded beyond his wildest dreams. By this time, Karen had finished drawing her illustration. Totally puzzled by the story and strange illustration, I suddenly realized that the drawing was of a large bird. "Hmmmm." Then it struck me. "A STORK!"

"You're PREGNANT!" I shouted.

"Yes! Yes!" Karen exclaimed, as tears of joy streamed down our faces.

Over dinner that evening, we discussed the timing of her pregnancy, and realized that she must have conceived right around the day, in fact, possibly on the very day, we had received the heartbreaking call from our pregnant friend's father.

"Timing," I mused. "What timing!"

Karen's face was glowing as she replied, "Was that a coincidence or WHAT!"

CHAPTER 8

ITCHY FINGER

Kima and Mwihila Missions - Western Province, Kenya, 1969

"It is not an accident for you to be present on earth in the twenty-first century. You are here now because the world needs the gifts you bring."

—Chris Michaels

Our departure date for Kenya was moved forward several weeks to allow for the advent of Rebekah Ruth, our daughter to be, to happen stateside. Teary-eyed grandparents did not diminish our excitement when they saw us off to New York, where we boarded the *Queen Elizabeth II* for the five-day voyage across the Atlantic, the second leg of the journey toward our ultimate destination, Kenya.

Standing on the stern of the celebrated "Lizzy," I felt a lump forming in my throat as we sailed slowly past the Statue of Liberty. Eight-weeks-old, bundled against the wind and the cold, and snuggled in Karen's arms, "Bekki" was totally oblivious to the emotions we were feeling, as the great American symbol of liberty and freedom began to fade in the distance.

Throughout the five-day voyage eastward, little Bekki's timetable got turned upside-down. She slept less each night of the crossing, until by the time we arrived, she was awake all night, and letting out intermittent screams, drowned out only by the droning of the vessel's incredibly loud engine, which surely was no further than a bulkhead away from our cramped little cabin below deck.

Flying out of London from Heathrow Aåirport, we arrived late and travel-weary in Nairobi, where we spent our first night. Late the next morning, there was a rapping on our door. It was our field secretary, Claire Shultz and his wife, Retha.

"How about some lunch, and then we'll head up country where we'll show you where you'll be living," Claire said.

Still a bit groggy, I replied, "We haven't even had breakfast yet."

"Okay, how about some brunch. We'll need to get going if we're going to get to the mission before dark."

Indeed, it *was* dark and raining hard by the time we reached the long hill that led to the mission. Claire was driving, and having trouble with the dirt road that had turned to pure mud. Finally unable to navigate through the mud, we found ourselves bogged down and stuck!

"David, let's get out and push, while Retha steers us up this hill."

As we finally gained some traction and reached the top of the hill, Retha stopped the car. She watched, as Claire and I climbed back in, with mud covering our bodies head to toe. Smiling, she said, "Welcome to Kenya."

Language study in Nairobi was rigorous, and sometimes embarrassing. For example, when our young Tanzanian teacher went around the room addressing each of us students with a question or statement in Swahili, she typically waited for a reasonable response in the same language. Her address to me was: "Habari gani?" which translates to "How are you"? or more accurately, "What's the news?"

34

My answer, after a thoughtful pause, was, "Ndizi," which I thought was the word for "Fine." To my embarrassment, amidst the laughter of the other students, I heard the teacher say, "No, No! 'Ndizi' means BANANAS!"

Also embarrassing to me, but I don't think to Karen, were the times when we could all plainly hear distinct slurping sounds from the back of the room, where Karen was nursing Bekki.

One day after we had been in Kenya a little over a year, Karen came home from a visit to the mission doctor with a telltale smile. I took one look at her and said, "Let me tell you...you're PREGNANT!"

"YES!"

The night Deborah Dawn was born at the mission hospital at Mwihila, the mood around that entire part of the country was enveloped in a kind of enraged mourning. That was the day Tom Mboya, the beloved, charismatic politician from that area, was buried, having been assassinated in Nairobi three days before. All the political indicators were pointing to the fact that this exceptionally popular politico would be giving President Kenyatta a very serious run in the upcoming presidential election. The fact that his assassins shot him down in broad daylight in downtown Nairobi caused no little political stir in Kenya, especially in our part of the country. Little did we know at the time, that the fact Debbi was born on the day of Tom Mboya's funeral *could*, very well, have affected what, by custom, we would name her.

Having lived in Western Kenya nearly two years, we were continuing to discover many of the fascinating traditions of that culture. The morning after Debbi was born we learned yet another one of the customs, when a young Kenyan male nurse asked Karen, "Is your baby a boy or a girl?"

Karen answered, "A girl," to which the young man

solemnly replied, "If she had been a boy, *you would have named him Tom Mboya*."

All the nurses and the two doctors living on the Mwihila Hospital compound were relieved when Debbi was born. Two weeks earlier, I had rushed Karen, on her due date, over the twenty-mile stretch of winding and rutted red dirt roads from Kima Mission to Mwihila in the middle of the night, because she was experiencing hard contractions. So fearful that the bumpy ride would bring on the baby before getting to the hospital, our Kima nurse decided to follow us, only to witness the termination of Karen's false labor upon our arrival at Mwihila.

Dr. Bill Anderson, the senior doctor at Mwihila, suggested that, under the circumstances, Karen should remain at Mwihila, anticipating her delivery any day. Two weeks later, while a farewell party was going on across the dirt road from the hospital for one of the departing missionaries, word was sent to the partying group that Karen's delivery was imminent. With that, the *entire party* of nurses, teachers and the two doctors went over to the hospital to welcome the new arrival.

Continuing in the celebratory spirit, Debbi entered the world to the accompaniment of a motley ad hoc choir made up of missionary teachers, medical staff, the delivering doctor, and the nervous father, all singing exuberantly at the top of our lungs the old hymn, "How Great Thou Art!"

Debbi was just eleven weeks old when we noticed little red spots beginning to appear on her abdomen, chest, back, legs, and arms. As the spots increased in number and size, and began to look like little pimples filled with puss, we took her back to Mwihila. Dr. Anderson was out that day, but the younger doctor, who was on duty, said it looked like chicken pox.

Several days passed and Debbi became increasingly restless, while her crying became more intense and frequent. About a week after her diagnosis, she had a particularly bad day. Debbi cried pretty much non-stop all day, except while nursing at Karen's breast. That night around eleven o'clock, while Karen was holding her and I was getting ready for bed, I took note of an itch on the index finger of my right hand. It had been itching and irritating me all day, but I had not really given it any particular attention. I looked at my itchy finger and noticed that just to the left of the nail, there was what looked like a pimple with a head on it that appeared to be ready to pop. I squeezed on it with the thumbnail of my left hand and out popped a little white worm. It took about two seconds for the horror of the situation to sink in. I rushed into the nursery where Karen was holding Debbi and squeezed on one of the spots on her body, and out popped a little white worm. Her tiny body was covered with worms! Frantically, we got Bekki up and over to a neighbor's house, and bundled up our precious baby for a rushed trip back to Mwihila. Our hearts were in our throats, as we traveled the twists and turns of the rutted dirt roads separating the two missions. We pulled into Dr. Anderson's driveway at midnight. I jumped out of the car, ran back to his bedroom window and started pounding on his window shouting, "Bill! Bill! Bill!" until I finally heard a sleepy, "Yes?"

"This is David!" I shouted. "Debbi is covered with worms!"

"Meet me at the hospital," came a suddenly wide-awake answer. The little mission hospital was down the hill and across the dirt road from the Anderson house. Dr. Anderson alerted a nurse and the two appeared a few minutes later in the hall where we were waiting. He pulled back the little blanket and took one knowing look at the tiny body—he had seen this condition many times before on African children—and asked us to wait there in the hall, as they disappeared into the operating theater.

The wait seemed like an eternity. I couldn't imagine how Debbi must have suffered with those dozens of worms under her skin, remembering how just one felt in my finger. What could she do but cry!

37

Finally, Dr. Anderson emerged and told us he had removed one hundred and four worms from various parts of her body. He added that he had administered just as much penicillin as her tiny body could tolerate. He said that it was critical that we had brought her in when we did and had not waited until morning. A few hours more might have been too late. Her prognosis was tenuous, but hopeful. The remainder of the night was long, as we kept vigil over our tiny bundle of humanity, flinching and squirming until she finally fell into a fitful sleep.

The next day, Dr. Anderson told us that these kinds of worms, commonly called mango worms, come from a certain kind of fly's eggs that sometimes get laid on clothing as they hang on the clothesline. These microscopic eggs are then transferred to the skin of the person wearing the clothing, where they become larvae; and if the skin is soft enough, as a child or baby's skin, they burrow in and begin to grow.

During the following days, as we watched Debbi's gradual recovery, we wondered *how* it could have happened, that one of those tiny larva could have possibly burrowed into my finger, pointing us, *in the nick of time*, to the devastation that was taking place in Debbi's body. As we look at Debbi today, whose body still bears the little scars from those near fateful days, and as we relate to her and love her, we are so very thankful for that one special little worm that somehow worked its way through my tough skin to give *me* that *itchy finger*.

CHAPTER 9

THE BRIDE

Kima Mission, Western Province, Kenya 1970
"Your spirit is eternal. Begin seeing yourself as a spiritual being
on a journey of discovery."

—Chris Michaels

Our final visit with my mother and father in their Florida home, before we left for Kenya, was bittersweet. Mother had not been feeling well, but I remember the tender love that showed in her face as she held little seven-week-old Bekki, rocking her in her favorite rocker. I wonder if Mother may have sensed then that she would not be around when we returned from Kenya following our four-year-term of service.

About a year after we arrived back in Kenya, we received a letter from Dad telling us of Mother's cancer. Six months later, another letter informed us of her passing. She had already been buried when we received the letter. Not being able to attend Mother's funeral and grieve with the rest of my family left me with feeling like a piece of myself had been torn away. What helped me most in my grieving was going to a little flower garden I planted in her memory, where I would think about her and meditate.

One night, the following year, I went to bed as usual. The next morning before waking, I had a dreamlike experience, unlike anything I had ever had before or since. I found myself in the old section of a town, where there were large, time-worn homes and huge majestic trees overhanging the sidewalk. I had the strange sensation of moving along in a kind of gliding motion, as if I were walking; but my feet were not touching the ground. Suddenly I was outside the town and entering a large pasture. Up ahead, I spotted an old hay wagon. When I got nearer the wagon, I noticed three little girls standing there. They were dressed in long, pretty dresses that appeared to be wedding outfits. I approached one of the girls and asked, in a think-talk, non-verbal kind of communication, "Where is the bride?"

The little girl replied, in the same non-verbal form of communication, "Around the other side of the wagon." Still in a kind of floating motion, I moved around to the other side of the wagon. There before me was what looked like a bride in an elegant, full-length, pure white wedding gown, with a veil covering her face. I moved beside the bride and said to the attendant behind her, using the non-verbal language, "Remove the veil." Slowly, the attendant pulled back the veil from the bride's face, and I found myself gazing into the face of my mother. She appeared young and beautiful, as she was years ago when I was a child. She did not see me, as her eyes were fixed straight ahead, as though she were looking expectantly for her groom. Stunned, I remained at her side, gazing into her face for what seemed like several seconds. Then, I abruptly found myself wide awake, sitting in an upright position in bed, with the distinct feeling I had just been in the presence of my mother.

Later that same day, I discovered, to my amazement, that Mother had passed away *exactly* one year before, *to that very day*. The emotion of the experience, plus the timing, convinced me that what I experienced that morning was not just an ordinary dream, but truly a gift to a young man who needed to see his mother one more time, before he could fully address and accept her passing.

CHAPTER 10

UH-OH!

Kima Mission, Western Province, Kenya 1970
"Since everything in this universe contains a spark of divinity,
everything plays a role in the divine plan."

—Yitta Halberstam and Judith Leventhal

Bekki was going on three years old, when we realized her language skills were not developing as they should. We inquired where we might find a speech therapist and were told there was only one speech therapist in the entire country, a Mrs. Couldry, a British lady who lived in Karen, a suburb of Nairobi. We contacted Mrs. Couldry and made arrangements to take Bekki twice a month to see her.

The journey to Karen involved an arduous seven-hour trip over rough, pot-holed roads, quite an ordeal just so Bekki could "go play" with her speech therapist. Mrs. Couldry organized the sessions so they were mostly for Karen and me—to teach us how to help Bekki learn to talk. She, at the same time, introduced powerful doses of a strong British accent, not only for Bekki, but for Karen and me, as well. Occasionally, we had to ask Mrs. Couldry after the session about a word or phrase she had used that we'd failed to understand, due to her prominent accent.

One time, at the end of a particularly grueling session, I asked her, "What is the meaning of 'kaa paak,' that you asked Bekki to repeat?" A mystified, then condescending look spread across her face, and she replied simply, "Why that's where you paak yoa kaa."

Mrs. Couldry inquired about our home life, after which she suggested part of Bekki's problem was she was hearing three different languages being spoken in our home: English, by Karen and me, as we spoke to each other; Swahili, which we spoke with Kenyans in and around the house; and Luyia, the tribal language she heard Kenyans speak to each other. And, oh yes, there was Mrs. Couldry's British English. Besides the confusion of the different languages Bekki heard, we discovered later she was also experiencing periodic fluid build-up in her ears; so whatever she was hearing much of the time was probably garbled.

At Christmas that year, Bekki and her little sister, Debbi, were the happy recipients of gifts sent from family and friends back home in the States. Bekki's favorite, by far, was her Chatty Cathy doll. Cathy could be prompted to say about twelve different phrases, like "Baby hungry," and "Mommy, I'm sleepy," by pulling a string that ran in and out of her back. Bekki would pull the string out and listen delightedly to Cathy "talking," as the string returned slowly into her back.

One day, Karen and I realized we had not seen Cathy for several days. When I asked Bekki where she was, she grabbed me by the pant leg and began pulling me toward the front door, down the front steps, and around to the corner of the house. There, we had a huge rain barrel that was used to catch water from off the roof. The barrel was perched up on a two and a half foot high concrete slab. Bekki stopped when we got to the barrel and pointed up at it, excitedly jabbering something I could not understand. Curious, I climbed up onto the concrete slab. As I peered down into the murky water, to my utter surprise, there was Cathy, face down, submerged just below the surface. Apparently, Bekki or one of her little friends, while they were playing, must have been twirling around and slung her up in the air and into the barrel. I reached down and lifted the hapless little doll out of the water. As I did, a constant stream of water came pouring out of her soaked, waterlogged body. Certain that she would never "speak" again, but still, on instinct, I took hold of the string and gave it a gentle pull. To my surprise, Cathy's string began coming out, a little jerky, but it continued coming out slowly until it suddenly stopped. A moment later, amazingly, it began making a steady, though choppy movement back into Cathy's body. Bekki and I waited with bated breath. The words were quivery but clear—"UH-OHHH... BAAAAABEEE WET!"

Those were the last, and no doubt, the most profound words Cathy ever uttered. I will never know, but I suspect that those final words spoken by little Chatty Cathy confirmed what Bekki knew all along, that Cathy always knew what she was talking about.

CHAPTER 11

Mother's Day

Bethlehem 1971

"I live and move and have my being in a universe that loves and supports me endlessly and infinitely."

—Leta Miller

I looked out of the hotel window and was surprised that it was light, being it was only 5:30 a.m. Down on the streets, Tel Aviv was already bustling with cars and people moving about. "It's Mother's Day," I thought. "What a perfect day to be visiting Bethlehem." Interestingly, although we had decided to spend a few days in Israel to visit some of the special sites, like Bethlehem, Jerusalem, and Nazareth, on our way back to the States, none of us had planned or foreseen we'd be visiting the birthplace of Jesus on Mother's Day.

As Karen and the girls were still asleep, I walked from the window over to the bed and looked down into Karen's face. She was sleeping peacefully on her back, and already showing that "Baby Number Three" was well on the way. I reached down and gently laid my hand on her tummy, just a centimeter or two from the tiny one resting inside. I thought to myself, "She or he will be blessed today, at the very place where Jesus was born."

The coastal city of Joppa (today known as Jaffa) had

always been, to me, just a place on an old map. Now, here it was, a busy modern city, but still with many reminders of the ancient world, like open markets and donkeys pulling carts. Our bus snaked through the narrow brick streets, evading meandering pedestrians and slow-moving donkeys. I recalled from reading the book of Acts in the Bible that a woman named Tabitha lived in Joppa, "a much loved woman who made clothes for the poor." Little did we know then, that the tiny one inside Karen would become a namesake of that beloved woman.

Leaving Joppa, we headed eastward through the Plains of Sharon, then gradually made the ascent, winding upward toward the ancient city of Jerusalem. We were surprised to learn that it was less than ten miles north of Bethlehem. It was a typical hot, dry Middle Eastern day, and the lack of greenery and the dust along the road were witnesses to it.

Karen placed her hand on her rounded tummy and reminisced, "Remember Mother's Day four and two years ago, when Bekki and Debbi were in my tummy?"

"I remember."

"You laid your hand here and blessed the one inside." Karen smiled.

"And we're going to do that again today. But this time, in a very special place."

Karen looked deeply into my eyes and nodded. "I can't believe we're actually going to see the place where Jesus was born," she said.

"Or at least where tradition says he was born," I added.

"Do you think the old stable is still there?" Karen questioned. "What about the inn? Or was he actually born in a cave, as some biblical authorities suggest?"

We were both surprised when the bus pulled up in front of an ancient church. The driver turned around in his seat and announced in his heavily accented voice,

46

"This is the Church of the Nativity. This is where Jesus was born."

Karen turned to me, "How can that be? There couldn't have been a church there when Jesus was born!"

The driver led the way, as we filed off the bus and toward the front of the church. Inside, the light was dim. The furnishings were ornate, having the appearance and musty smell of being very old. The driver called out for us to follow him over to where there was a stairway leading down into the lower part of the church. There was even less fresh air and light, as we made our way slowly down the stairwell. When we all reached the bottom of the stairs, the driver called out, "Come!"

Those at the head of the group trudged along behind him, as we moved deeper into the undercroft. Karen and I purposefully fell back to the end of the group. The line of people moved slowly, stopped, and then began moving again. Finally, we entered an area that was well lighted. I looked around and saw we were in what looked like an underground room, which could easily have been just a cave two thousand years ago. There, in a kind of enclave, behind a large, protective glass, was a rustic looking manger with an infant doll lying in it. The four of us stood transfixed. I thought to myself, "Yes, this could have been the place." We waited until the last tourist left the area. I then placed my hand on Karen's tummy and prayed God's blessing on the unborn child.

We didn't speak as we walked outside into the fresh air and bright sunlight; then Karen turned to me and said, "It seems like the most significant things that happen to us are those things that we don't plan."

CHAPTER 12

DESERT ANGEL

Khartoum to Aswan 1976

"For he will give his angels charge of you to guard you in all your ways.
On their hands they will bear you up, lest you dash your foot against a stone."

—Psalm 91:11-12

We'd been thinking a lot about home, as the end of our term was drawing near, and how we might travel to get there. We had lived in Africa over a period of ten years, and had adjusted to the culture and the overall slowed-down pace of life. While Karen and I were thinking about ourselves and wondering how we were going to adjust to the fast-paced American way, what about our little girls, who were just five, seven, and nine, who knew nothing but the African way of life? Realizing that, we were a little freaked out at the thought of just getting on a plane and suddenly landing in a culture and a way of life that was so vastly different from what we had enjoyed over the past ten years.

One day while talking about how we might get back to our native America, the idea emerged that what we could do is work our way back gradually overland through north Africa and Europe, and finally to Amsterdam, where we would board a plane for our splashdown in America.

Once we had convinced ourselves this was the way we wanted to go, we started talking to our friends about it. Most of them were taken aback with the thought of taking off on such an adventure, especially with three little girls going overland through northern Africa. I remember the words of one of our friends: "You're crazy."

Ignoring all the well-intentioned advice of our friends, we proceeded with our plans. We did, however, check with the American Embassy about our proposed trip. At the Embassy, we met with one of the officers and told him our plans. He listened thoughtfully, then said, "You can't go overland through Ethiopia, because there is fighting going on there right now. What you *can* do is fly out of Nairobi to Khartoum, then go overland from there." Karen and I were somewhat disappointed, but we agreed to follow his recommendations.

One evening, we were having dinner with some friends at the Mennonite Guest House. A meal there was always a special treat, not only because of the delicious Mennonite foods they served, but it seemed they always had an especially interesting guest or two staying there. That evening was no exception. There was a man at our table who was a small plane pilot with several years' experience flying in and around Africa. I told him about our planned trip out of Africa overland from Khartoum northward to Wadi Halfa, Aswan, and points north to Alexandria.

He listened with interest, and then, wiping his mouth with a napkin, said, "I'm familiar with that area. I flew into Wadi Halfa once. It's just south of the border between the Sudan and Egypt, you know. The temperature at the time I was there was 132 degrees, but let me tell you," he continued, "in Aswan, there's a German hostel where you can stay on your way through. They're nice folks. You can write to them, and make a reservation. I happen to have their address in my bag. Here, I'll get it for you."

When we got home later that evening, I drafted a letter to them and dropped it in the mail the next day. During the following weeks, however, we never heard anything back.

Our Mennonite friends put us in touch with another Mennonite family named Baumann who lived in Khartoum, whom, they said, might be a good contact for us. I wrote to them, and received a letter right back saying they would be happy to pick us up at the airport, and take us to their home, where we could stay during our time in Khartoum. Interestingly, while Karen's maiden name is Baumann, our research didn't reveal where there might be a family relationship.

"We'll be landing in Khartoum in approximately five minutes. Please fasten your safety belts," came a crackly announcement over the airplane's intercom. We looked out the window. All we could see was more of the same vast desert we'd been looking at for the last hour or so. Minutes later, we spotted a wide river running northward, then another river coming into view from the east, merging with the one running north. Remembering my geography, I knew what we were looking at.

Look," I said, "that's the Nile River. The one we saw first, running northward, is the White Nile. See how slowly it's moving, coming from its source, Lake Victoria, in Uganda. Now, see how fast the river coming from the east is moving. That's the Blue Nile, and it's tumbling down off the high mountains of Ethiopia."

"That's amazing," Karen said. "Look how wide the river is now, and how the left half of it is moving so slowly, yet the right side is moving fast." As we circled to make our landing, we saw that the city was completely surrounded by nothing but vast deserts as far as the eye could see. It made me wonder how it might feel to live there, like living in a city imprisoned by a wall of desert.

Inside the airport, we were approached by a nice-looking young man. He smiled and said, "I'll bet you are the Crippens. I'm Charles Baumann. It was easy to identify you, with the three girls trailing along behind. This is my wife, Fern. Welcome to Khartoum."

That evening at supper, Fern said, "We sleep on our roof here in Khartoum. It's a flat roof, and everybody sleeps on their roofs. It's just too hot in the house. It's amazing how the temperature drops at night, and we get a little breeze up there."

Charles broke in, "Tomorrow, we'll take you to where you can purchase your tickets for the train to Wadi Halfa. From there, a truck will carry you to the Nile, where a boat pulling a barge will take you up the river to Aswan."

"Some of our friends have taken that route," Fern added, "and they've all warned us to be sure and tell anyone else going that way to carry lots and lots of water, because it's a three-day journey and the only water that's available is not safe to drink."

Bekki, Debbi, and Tabbi were intrigued, looking out over the side of the roof at the neighbors on their roofs, as they were spreading out their sleeping gear on the surrounding roofs, getting ready for a cool night's sleep."

One thing we noticed about Khartoum was that the vast majority of the people were Arabs. There seemed to be few blacks, and rarely did we see the face of a European or American on the streets. The day before we were to leave by train for Wadi Halfa, while the five of us were out walking along the shops, we noticed a tall, attractive woman with long blond hair coming in our direction. As she was so neatly dressed, at first glance I thought she must be an executive from a large corporation doing business in Khartoum. I was surprised when, instead of walking past us, she suddenly stepped straight over to us, and with a foreign accent I couldn't quite place, said, "Excuse me, but are you going to Wadi Halfa?"

Responding to her question, I said, "As a matter of fact, we are."

She then introduced herself, saying, "My name is

Oolah." After pausing, she added, "May I travel with you?"

Just to say we were surprised would be an understatement. For one thing, she looked like a person who would be flying first class on a jet plane, and not going the hard way, like we had chosen. However, Karen and I looked at each other, and together said, "Yes." Then I added, "Of course you can go with us. Why not?"

"Well, then, may we walk over to the train station, so I can purchase my ticket? It's just a few blocks that way," she said, pointing.

At the station, Oolah turned to Karen and me, and said, "It's against the law, here in the Sudan, for a woman to travel alone without her husband." Looking directly at me, she said, "So, could I go with you...as your second wife?"

Speechless, I looked at Karen. Finally, with a little shrug, Karen said, "Why not?"

Oolah then handed me a small wad of cash and I purchased the ticket for "my second wife."

"The train leaves at 6:00 a.m.," the ticket man said, as he handed me the ticket.

"I will meet you here at the station in the morning at six," she said. We all watched open-mouthed, as she walked away.

Supper that evening featured a delicious goat stew. "I'm afraid you don't have enough containers for all the water you will need for drinking," Fern said. "The water on the train and on the boat is not safe to drink; and you will be traveling for three days by train and boat to Aswan. We'll fill all your containers with water after supper, and give you two more containers that we aren't using any more."

We arrived at the station a few minutes before six the next morning to find a train with an engine and wooden coaches that looked like something out of the TV show,

Petticoat Junction, only not quite so shiny. I could already feel the heat of the early morning sun bearing down, as we climbed on board and found our compartment already occupied by three Arab women and several small children. A few Arab men were standing in the narrow passageway just outside the compartment. The women made a friendly gesture of squeezing together with their children to make room for us to sit down.

Six o'clock came and no Oolah. Finally, just as the train jerked and began to move, in came Oolah with a big box balanced on her shoulder. She had dressed down for the trip, and we could see the strength in her arms. We looked on curiously, as she set the box down where we could see an assortment of liquor and wine bottles.

"We're going to need a lot of water," she explained, "so last night I went around to all the nicer hotel bars and collected empty bottles and filled them with good drinking water."

The train gradually picked up speed, and we were soon out in the desert. All we could see from the open window was sand and a few scrub bushes here and there. As the sun rose higher, the temperature rose accordingly. The open window was letting in very hot air mixed with swirling clouds of dust and sand. I decided to close the window, but quickly found that the heat was so stifling, it was unbearable. We settled for a partially open window, dust and all. I noticed there didn't seem to be any perspiration on me or anyone in the compartment. Apparently, it simply evaporated before it formed.

As the morning wore on, we found ourselves drinking water constantly, trying in vain to quench our thirsts. At the end of our coach was a large clay jar in a wooden frame that had been filled with water. People were dipping into it with their tin cups, and some with their bare hands. Considering what kind of germs, bacteria and viruses were getting into that water, I was beginning to realize that maybe my "second wife" was with us to save our lives.

Sometime in the late morning, the train slowed down and gradually came to a jerky stop. We looked out the window, expecting to see at least a small train station. There was nothing, only sand and some low, dried out desert brush. People were getting off and heading for those few bushes they could find and then returning to the train. We finally decided that this was our chance to do the same, so we did. Shortly after we got back on board, the train jerked and started moving again. Not long after our brief stop, I noticed one of the little Arab girls, who must have missed getting off earlier, straddling one of our cloth bags of food. I thought she was going to sit down on it. But instead of sitting, she squatted, and let loose a yellow stream.

By afternoon, I began to wonder how we were ever going to sleep that night, as we were all squashed together so tightly. Even with most of the children on the floor, there was no way we adults could stretch out. Just as the desert sun was setting, casting a luminous glow across the spacious sands, the train began to slow down and finally came to a stop. The three Arab women in our compartment picked up their bags, gathered their children, and with shy waves and a few words we did not understand, left, following the three men who had been sitting on the floor outside our compartment. Our stop in the little desert town of Atbara was brief. As we began moving again, we heaved a big sigh of relief, and spread out a mat on the floor, where our three girls were happy to lay their tired bodies down for the night.

The desert night descended, and all the light we could see was from the one dim bulb in our compartment. Oolah, Karen, and I were all exhausted from the heat and ready to bed down; but, of course, there were only two wooden bench seats facing each other, and our already matted-down girls filled the floor space between. "You and Karen sleep on the bench seats," Oolah said, "and I'll climb up onto the baggage rack, where you can then strap me in with some rope I have in my bag."

"No, no!" I protested, "I'll go up on the baggage rack

and you strap *me* in."

But Oolah had already climbed up and was handing me her rope. I strapped it around her body, securing her firmly to the rack. I left her arms free, but otherwise she had very little wiggle room. I asked, "How do you feel?"

"Snug."

Those were the final words spoken in the dim light of our little compartment. I took a deep breath. Stepping carefully around our sleeping little girls, I closed the window, only to realize that it was still deathly hot with it closed; so I opened it again, letting in the hot air and dust.

We awoke the next morning completely covered with thick, gray dust. As I gazed at the lot of us, we looked like a family of ghosts!

It was noon when we pulled into the tiny station of Wadi Halfa, and our water supply was exhausted. What was left were several bottles of Oolah's water. Standing in line under the scorching sun to get our passports stamped, I remembered the words of the pilot we had met at the Mennonite Guest House. "Yes, it has to be at least 132 degrees," I mused.

Several trucks that looked like dump trucks were standing by, which I supposed were the vehicles that would be transporting us over to the Nile. I noticed there was no road leading west toward the great river, just the gentle rolling hills of pure sand. We boarded one of the trucks along with other passengers, mostly Arabs, as the drivers gunned their engines, gearing up to head out into the open desert. After about an hour of churning through the trackless sand, I began getting nervous, and started to wonder if we were lost. I stared out across the horizon, squinting my eyes. Almost as though it were an answer to my prayers, I could see what looked like an old steam ship with a barge attached. At last, I'd caught sight of the river in the distance!

Since our tickets were for the barge, we were a little

concerned to find what looked like an endless stream of Africans already crowding onto the barge. We learned later they were refugees fleeing Chad, due to the war going on there. We got in line and climbed aboard, and were immediately assured there was no water on board that was safe for us to drink. Following what we saw others doing, we staked out just enough space for all six of us to lie flat by spreading out our mats and putting all our bags around the edges as a kind of barricade against the teeming mass of bodies that were in constant motion around us. Unfortunately, we soon realized why that particular spot had been left open. It was squarely on the path to the only toilet on the barge!

It was mid-afternoon, and the sun was brutally beating down upon us, once again. Finally, a whistle blew, the ropes securing the boat and the barge to the dock were released, and we began moving slowly up the Nile. Not long after we were cut loose from the dock, we noticed our girls getting acquainted with several of our Arab neighbors who were sharing small cups of tea with them and with a young white man, whom we later learned was suffering from hepatitis. As the sun sank lower in the western sky, a gentle breeze swept mercifully across the barge, providing a brief, but welcome respite to the intense heat. Karen pulled our small, one-burner stove and the makings for supper out of our bags and began preparing the meal. When we eventually began eating, a young Australian hippie couple came over and offered to let our girls sleep with them. "We have a spot over there next to the bulkhead that is safer than here," the young man said, pointing. "The chance of getting stepped on in the middle of the night is less likely."

"Let us go!" Debbi piped up.

I looked over to the spot the young couple had staked out. It was just about fifteen feet away. "Okay."

Karen looked concerned, but then nodded to the couple, "Thanks."

The next morning, as we caught sight of the Aswan

dam, our throats were parched and Oolah's water was down to just a few drops. When our feet finally hit solid ground, as we disembarked at the dam, we knew relief for our lack of water was in sight.

"By the way," I said to Karen, "where's Oolah?"

"I don't know. I thought she was with us when we were getting off the barge." I asked our girls. They said they hadn't seen her.

Indeed, we never saw Oolah again. Our desert angel was gone.

CHAPTER 13

THE GERMAN CONNECTION

Aswan 1976

*"Synchronicities and so-called coincidences are clear signs that
the Divine Source is knocking on your door."*

—John Holland

Aswan was a welcome sight. "Let's find the nearest shop where we can find something to drink," we heard one of our fellow travelers say. Most of the twelve or so hippie types were hanging together, and we followed along. One who seemed to know his way around Aswan led us to a café, where we all swarmed in and drank as much liquid as our stomachs would hold.

"Where are you guys spending the night?" I asked.

"I was here once before," one of the young men responded. "The youth hostel is a good place to stay, and it's close-by."

"Sounds good to me," I answered.

We were unpacking our bags on the second floor of the youth hostel, when Karen said, "You know, the Aga Khan mausoleum is just across the river from here. I would really like to go see it while we're here. I asked the man at the desk, and he said it's just a short camel ride after a boat trip across the river."

59

"Well, why don't you go for it, if you have the strength. I'll stay here with the girls. I'm whipped."

Debbi, who had been lying tummy down on her bunk from the time we arrived, popped her head up, and said, "I want to go."

"Fine," I said, looking at Karen for her agreement. "I'll stay here with Bekki and Tabbi."

By this time Bekki and Tabbi were complaining of stomach upset, and I was feeling more than a bit rough myself.

When they returned, I received the following report from Karen.

She and Debbi had just arrived at the mausoleum when Debbi began feeling sick, and started throwing up. Karen felt her forehead, and found she was burning up with fever. They rushed out of the mausoleum and took the next camel ride back to the river. Soon, they were on a small boat headed for the Aswan side. The boat had a large sail, but moved along slowly, as the wind was down. Karen reached over the side, and getting water in her cupped hand, poured the cooling water over Debbi's head. This temporarily helped cool down our little girl.

On the Aswan side, there is a cliff and a very steep climb from the bottom up to the street level. Karen looked at the steep climb as the boat pulled up to shore, and had no idea how she could ever get Debbi up the steps. Suddenly, she caught sight of a man walking toward them. He looked like an Egyptian, dressed in the traditional long white jalabia. Without saying a word, the man reached down and gathered Debbi up into his arms, lifting her out of the boat, and began walking up the steep steps, with Karen following closely behind. At the top of the stairs, on the street, he headed toward the youth hostel, walking slowly and saying nothing. When he reached the youth hostel, he proceeded in and walked up the stairs to the second floor, where he laid her down gently onto a cot. Karen pulled money from her pocket and handed it to him. His dramatic hand motions made it clear to her that he would not accept any money, as he turned and disappeared down the stairs.

"Debbi's sick and has a high fever!" Karen said to me, after the man had left.

I could see the urgency in her eyes. I felt Debbi's head, and ran down the stairs.

"Where can we take a very sick child?" I asked the man behind the counter.

"Across town, there is a hospital. You take her there. You will find a cart pulled by a donkey around the side of our building. He will get you to the hospital."

We found the donkey cart, just as the man had said, and within minutes we and all our baggage were on a slow trek across town. Thirty minutes later, we stopped in front of what looked like a large white house, and the driver turned to face us. Pointing up at the building, he said, "Hospital."

Once we got to the front door, I pushed the doorbell and we all stood there with our baggage piled up around us, waiting for someone to answer. Shortly, the door was opened by a middle-aged woman dressed in white and wearing a nurse's cap.

"Hello," I said, "My name is David Crippen, and this is my family, and one of our little girls..."

"Oh, the Crippens!" she interrupted, with a heavy German accent. "Where have you been? We've been looking for you."

Shocked, we looked at each other in amazement. Then Karen remembered the letter I had written two months earlier, to what we thought was a German hostel, where we thought we might stay.

"You wrote to us several weeks ago," she said.

"Yes, we were told there was a hostel here where we might stay," I replied.

"Oh, never mind, come in! You all look dreadfully

tired!"

"Well, we are, but little Debbi, here, suddenly got very sick today...and we were told to come here."

She placed her hand on Debbi's head, looked at Karen, and said, "Yes, yes, this child has a high fever. Follow me. We have an empty room down the hall."

She led us to a room that had all the appearances of having been prepared especially for us. It was large with two beds, and much to our relief, was cool and clean. Everything was white, and to our delight, this included crisp, white sheets and fluffy pillows.

We had not been there more than thirty minutes when a younger, pretty, round- faced nurse came to our room with a tray holding five glasses of cool, freshly squeezed orange juice. Things seemed to be shaping up better, at that point.

On our third day there, the nurse who had let us in came to our room and said, "Your little Debbi has typhoid fever. We will have to keep you here for at least a few more days."

The typhoid fever was a shocker; but the thought of staying there a few more days came as good news, because all of us were still feeling more than a little puny.

We remained there in the loving care of the German nurses for an entire week, where we received excellent medical treatment from each of them and from a young Egyptian doctor.

After a week, we packed our bags and I asked how much we owed them for our stay.

"Oh, you don't owe us a thing; and by the way, we have a car and will take you to the train station, where you'll be off to Cairo."

We were about to board the train, when the German woman who drove us to the station opened her purse, and handed me a small bundle of cash, saying, "In our prayer meeting last night, we took up a little offering for you. We hope this will help you along your way."

Once we got our three girls and our baggage on board, and seated ourselves, our heads were still spinning over all that had happened since we'd left Khartoum.

After several minutes of quiet, except for the rhythmic clickidy-clack sound of the wheels on the track, Karen broke the silence. "Remember the pilot we met at the Mennonite Guest House that night two months ago?"

"Yeah, I sure do."

"Where would we be now, if we hadn't met him?"

I thought about that for a minute. "Yeah, and where would we be if Oolah hadn't come along, and if we hadn't been directed to the German hospital?"

I took a deep breath and settled back into my seat. Suddenly, a resounding feeling of "all is well" washed over me. I quietly stared out the window, and drifted peacefully into a deep sleep.

CHAPTER 14

KEE-MAH

Lakeland, Florida - Bangkok 1980
"I've seen love from both sides now.
It's everywhere, Amen, bow-wow..."

—Wendy Francisco

The girls wanted a dog and, after our recent episode with a cat, Karen and I were *ready* for a dog. A couple of months earlier, a rather large cat had followed the girls home from school and immediately settled herself down in the middle of our living room. By the time I got home, four kittens had already been delivered and four more were on the way. The final number of furry little newborns matched the number of kids who had somehow been magnetically drawn into our living room from all over the neighborhood to watch this "spectacle of nature." As it turned out, we were able to find homes for each of the kittens, as well as the "mom-cat."

Following a lead from a newspaper ad, the five members of our family soon found ourselves in a home across town looking at a small, white, curly haired dog that the owners said was a Peekapoo. The young couple was moving to an apartment where dogs were not allowed, and I remember the lady of the house crying as we walked out with their dog. They had named her Lambchop, a name I liked and thought suited her very well. But, of course, the girls had their own ideas about naming. All the way home in the backseat of our VW bug, they called out all the names they could think of until, finally, one of them said, "Kima." Kima was the name of the mission station in Kenya where Bekki had spent her first four years, where we were living when Debbi was born, and where Tabbi was conceived—all of which somehow added up to making it just the perfect name for our new dog.

Four years had passed since our return to America, after living overseas for ten years, and we were finally beginning to feel at home in our own culture. I was working in a newly opened close security state prison just outside of Lakeland. My job responsibility was to organize and run the education program. I found this work extraordinarily fulfilling—helping to give those who had made some bad choices in their lives a second chance to gain a level of dignity and self respect. Karen too was feeling a sense of satisfaction and fulfillment as a social worker in an alternative school.

We had just purchased a modest three-bedroom house that came with a lake across the street where the girls could swim—that is, until one day, I spotted an alligator less than thirty feet from them in the water. Add the proverbial family station wagon and the new dog to the picture and one might easily guess our family had settled in for the duration.

One evening shortly after Kima joined our household, there came a sharp rapping on our front door, followed by a barrage of high-pitched barks. Very quickly, Kima had, indeed, become the chief protector of her three young charges.

"Karen and Charlie Smith!" I said, greeting two of our favorite people standing in our doorway. "Who turned you loose, and what are you doing in our neck of the woods?"

"Just a funny set of circumstances," Charlie responded with a big grin.

"Yeah, we had a scheduled meeting here in Lakeland, or so we thought," Karen chimed in, "but when we arrived, nobody was there. I guess it had been rescheduled and we didn't know it."

"So," Charlie said, "we thought, well, as long as we're here in Lakeland with nothing going on, why not go pester the Crippens."

"Well, don't just stand there, come on in!" my Karen exclaimed.

The year before, Charlie and I had taught together in the same college and had become best friends. He and his Karen, who was a registered nurse, were in Malaysia with the Peace Corps, while we were in training to go there. If we had gone ahead with Peace Corps work as we had hoped, we would have no doubt met the Smiths there; but, as it was, we ended up meeting them in college 11 years later. Apparently we were destined to meet somewhere.

For the first thirty minutes of Karen and Charlie's visit, our living room rocked with laughter, as we reminisced about all the good times we'd shared together before the miles separated us.

Then, Charlie said, "Oh, let me tell you about the job we're being offered. You may have heard of Food for the Hungry. It's an international relief and development organization whose primary purpose is to go into areas where there's massive starvation and severe malnutrition. Right now, they need a director in Thailand to head up the feeding program they're operating along the border. They're feeding refugees who are pouring across the borders from Cambodia and Laos, *plus* boat people coming in from Vietnam. It sounds exciting and we'd love to do it, but we've about decided the timing is just not right for us, at least not right now."

I listened with interest as he described what they were being asked to consider. Then, the conversation shifted to lighter things for the remainder of the evening.

Finally, Charlie looked at his watch and said, "We'd better get going, before we're too sleepy to drive." We all got up and Karen and I followed them to the door.

Halfway out the door, Charlie's Karen turned and said, "You know, I think this thing Charlie and I've been asked to do has the *Crippen* name on it."

"You know," Charlie added, "the Vice President of Food for the Hungry, Ells Culver, is flying here in just a few days to meet with us. If you are even the *slightest* bit interested, come on over and meet Ells."

Ells was already at the Smith house, talking about Food for the Hungry and their need for a director in Thailand, when Karen and I walked in. Over a scrumptious dinner of Charlie's famous chicken curry, we listened to Ells describe in detail what Food for the Hungry was doing in the refugee camps. After dessert, Ells looked at Karen and me and said, "Charlie told me they have a rowboat tied up at their dock behind the house that's available. Would you like to go for a little ride out in the lake? I'll row."

The moon was bright and nearly full, and its light danced across the ripples in the lake. As we continued our conversation about Thailand and the need for new leadership there, Ells said, "David, if you and Karen are interested in the possibility of taking on the work there, I would like to fly you to Thailand to give you a firsthand look at what we're doing there, after which we can talk some more about it."

Six weeks later, we were in the air on our way to Thailand, Kima and all. Shortly after arriving in Bangkok, we moved into a house and hired two young Thai women named Took and Peepah to cook, clean, and look after the house while we were at work. Both the young women were shy, especially Peepah. They didn't speak any English and we were just beginning to learn Thai; so, almost all communication had to be done using sign language.

Karen, right away, took on the job of feeding Kima

every morning before we left for work, and every evening after getting home.

One evening while Karen was out front calling, "Kima, Kima, come get your supper," she noticed Took and Peepah standing nearby with their hands over their mouths giggling. After that, she noticed that every time she called, "Kima," Took and Peepah covered their mouths, looked at each other, and giggled. Finally, Karen realized that the word "Kima" must mean something very special in Thai.

She was taking a Thai language class at the time; so at her next session, she asked her young Thai teacher what "Kima" meant in Thai. The moment Karen said, "Kima," he covered his mouth and blushed.

"Well, what does it mean?" she asked.

"I cannot tell you."

She asked again, and he just turned away and said, "I can't say."

Finally, after much prodding, he said, "Well, '*mah*' means *dog*, and '*kee*' means..." and he stopped, too embarrassed to go on.

At last he said, "Kee...is what a dog leaves out in the grass."

Horrified, Karen realized that all this time she had been standing out in the front yard hollering, "DOG SHIT! DOG SHIT!"

CHAPTER 15

POLISH SURPRISE

Bangkok 1980

"How the information arrives is always a mystery. Usually, it comes to us through another human being, either in her words or through her actions. It can also come in the form of a book, magazine, or news item."

—James Redfield

Took and Peepah had been cooking for us just less than a week when I became convinced I was tasting the same spice or flavoring or *something* in our scrambled eggs and in most everything else they cooked. It was a taste I could not tolerate and one to which I knew I would never adjust. Whatever it was they were mixing into our food was, to me, unbearable.

We had been warned during our brief orientation to the Thai culture of the sensitive feelings we might encounter in our house help, so I decided to move with caution regarding how to investigate what was being added to our food that must be so delightful to the Thai taste. One little barrier to my planned investigation was the fact that I had learned very few words in Thai; actually, just enough that if I tried to say anything, it would probably only make matters worse. What made it so tricky was that Thai is a tonal language; so if, for instance, you say a word that sounds like 'cow' to the

American ear, to the Thai, you might be saying any of nine different words including "rice," "hill," or "knee."

One evening, determined to solve the mystery of the ill-tasting food, I positioned myself just inside the kitchen door, while Took and Peepah were cooking dinner. Watching them like a hawk, I very soon discovered my first mistake was just being in the kitchen. Even though they were younger than I, and while I was the one paying the rent for the house (which of course included the kitchen), I somehow got the feeling they felt the kitchen belonged to them. Somehow their body language suggested to me that I just didn't belong there; but, nevertheless, I was determined to stay there until the culinary mystery was solved.

Just then, I spotted a strange substance being poured into a pot on the stove. I walked over to investigate and as politely as possible, coaxed the bottle of brownish liquid out of Took's hand and started to put it to my nose, thus committing the unpardonable sin. Before even getting it all the way up to my nose, I knew *this* was the culprit. As tactfully as possible, using my most respectful sign language, I told them *never* to put *that* substance into any of our food again. The look of shock, horror, and utter disbelief on Took's face literally drove me out of the kitchen, a territory I never invaded again, while occupied by the two women.

I learned later that what I had found so offensive was "fish sauce," a food source, we were told, most Thais add to many of their dishes. It is made from the droppings of fish that are salted and hung out until they ripen.

One of the persons who no doubt helped us navigate through the bumps and pitfalls of working in the Thai culture was a bright and energetic mature woman named Adelia Bernard. Adelia was originally from Yugoslavia and was a first cousin to Mother Teresa, a claim that I had no trouble believing, not only because of her deep commitment to people who were the most needy, but also because of her eyes and the configuration of her face that brightened her entire countenance when she smiled, mirroring the likeness of the famous modern-day saint. Adelia assisted in our Bangkok office, but what she enjoyed most was traveling out to the refugee camps, getting to know the refugees, and working with our teams preparing and distributing food. Her gregarious and loving spirit made her a favorite among countless refugees.

Besides being a deeply spiritual person, Adelia had all the social protocol skills necessary to navigate her way around several embassies, government agencies, and non-government organizations where she went often to speak out on behalf of refugee issues.

One day shortly before Christmas, I received a phone call in my office from Adelia. She announced that she had two Polish couples with her who had just escaped from behind the Iron Curtain. Those were Cold War days with the Soviet Union, when people who lived on the east side of the "Iron Curtain," which stretched across Eastern Europe, risked their lives to escape from Soviet-dominated countries like Poland.

The two couples, she said, had made a dangerous, but successful escape after many months of careful planning. They had just arrived in Bangkok and she had spent the day taking them around to the Australian Embassy, the American Embassy, the UNHCR, and the office of the International Committee of the Red Cross, pleading for some help for them. After explaining all this, she asked if she could bring them to our house for dinner that evening. I agreed, and asked one of our Thai staff to call Took, to ask her to prepare a nice meal for all of us.

When we arrived home that evening the miracle began to unfold. In the day's mail waiting for us was a small package from a woman named Gaye Ciesinski, who was herself of Polish descent. Two years earlier, as the Education Supervisor at the prison where I worked, I had hired Gaye as a teacher, and since then we had kept in touch with each other. I was standing on the front porch, unwrapping the little package, when I looked up and saw a taxi pulling up in front of the house. I watched as Adelia and the two Polish couples, together with two young children, got out of the taxi. As they made their way up the sidewalk, I quickly finished unwrapping the package, only to discover, to my astonishment, that the package contained a cassette tape of *Polish Christmas carols*, along with their Christmas greeting.

Stunned by what I was holding in my hands, and the timing of the whole thing, my face must have looked like I had just experienced a divine visitation. Greetings were exchanged in English and Polish, and I gestured our guests into the house and to a comfortable sofa and chairs across from the speakers of our cassette tape player.

Without a word, I popped the tape into the stereo and sat down. Momentarily, the room swelled with the most beautiful music I had ever heard—the rich, sweet voices of an extraordinary Polish choir singing the carols of Christmas.

Captivated by the miracle of the moment, I glanced over at the couples sitting across from me. Tears were streaming down their cheeks. At the end of the tape, Adelia, who spoke enough Polish to interpret, told us that because the Communist government they had been living under for so long did not allow the playing of Christian Christmas carols on the radio, they had not heard those carols sung since they were children.

How was it that Gaye Ciesinski was moved to send that little package when she did, and how was it that it was opened at that precise moment?

CHAPTER 16

BLESSED

Bangkok 1981

". . . everywhere we are, every minute of our lives, Spirit is right there with us, ready to move into our experience with all Its power and goodness, the moment we provide the outlet."

—Ron Fox

Driving in Bangkok traffic at rush hour may best be compared to trying to maneuver your way through a stampede of cattle in slow-motion; except, instead of breathing in dust, you are taking in a bluish haze of automotive emissions. Half the time is spent stalled with the engine idling, and the other half creeping through the mass of cars, motorcycles, tuk-tuks (three-wheeled motorized taxis), and buses, all belching out exhaust fumes, which rise up to form the thick cloud hanging over the perpetual tangle of vehicles like a full-blown thundercloud. The typical morning run from our house to our downtown office was forty minutes.

Someone from our staff of four Thais and seven Americans would always have coffee brewing by the time we arrived, and our work day always began with the reading of a portion of scripture, followed by a few words of commentary and prayer.

One morning, while still at home, I decided I would

begin our morning session with the reading of a portion of Jesus' Beatitudes, which all start with the word "blessed." I wanted to begin by saying something about the meaning of the word "*blessed*;" but the more I thought about it, the more I realized I really did not know exactly what it meant. For instance, what does "blessed" mean when Jesus says, "*Blessed* are those who grieve, for they shall be comforted;" or when he says, "*Blessed* are the merciful, for they shall receive mercy;" or "*Blessed* are the peacemakers, for they shall be called children of God"? I wanted a single definition of the word and I wasn't getting it. I mentioned this to Karen and she was not very helpful.

As we left the house to begin our trek through the morning traffic, I was still struggling with the meaning of the word. While stalled in the middle of a snarl of vehicles, all waiting for the lone traffic cop to wave us on, and still trying to come up with a satisfactory definition, I noticed some writing on the rear window of the small, older sedan directly in front of us. Strangely enough, it was in *English*. When I read what it said, I was dumbfounded! Hardly believing what I was reading, and wanting to confirm what I was seeing, I said to Karen (who was in the passenger seat beside me), "Look at the rear window of that car in front of us and read to me what it says."

Karen looked at the words, then looked at me in utter disbelief. Slowly, word by word, she read aloud, *BLESSED = PEACE AND JOY TOGETHER.*

CHAPTER 17

TERROR IN THE RICE PADDIES

Thailand 1982

"If we did not believe that God had an 'interest' in us, so to speak, or that we had direct access to Universal Power, how could we begin anything, when faced with some of the obstacles in our lives?"

—Margaret Stortz

We had been warned more than once of the marauders who roamed one particular stretch of road running through many lonely miles of rice paddies. This was a road we traveled often, which ran between Bangkok and Shrok Shrong, a small village just inside the Cambodian border, where we teamed with another agency to do medical work and supplementary feeding. These "bandits on motorcycles" had chosen this road because, at night, one could travel for many miles in total darkness and there was no human habitation along the way. It was not at all uncommon to hear of robberies, beatings, and even murders of innocent travelers on that particular highway. Of course, we were careful to travel through there only during the daylight hours, when there were at least a few other vehicles on the road.

One day, though, we had carelessly remained in the Cambodian village later than usual, and the darkness caught us before we got to that area. Traveling with us

77

that evening were our friends, Father Boonlert, a Thai Catholic priest; Adelia; Rhonda, Bekki's tutor; and three of our refugee workers. Our little yellow Toyota van (which we affectionately called the "Yellow Submarine"), had always performed perfectly on our trips back and forth to the border camps and, as far as we knew, was still in excellent running order.

By the time we got to the no-man's-land portion of the trip, the darkness had settled over us like a black upside-down bowl. We were about halfway through the pitch-black, two-lane road, when suddenly the engine started skipping and we gradually began losing speed. I was at the wheel and knew we had many miles to go before getting into a populated area. The skipping got worse and I began having to nurse the accelerator peddle, just to maintain a speed of twenty to thirty miles per hour. We all began straining our eyes across the flat horizon of rice paddies, searching for any light that might be penetrating the deep darkness. Father Boonlert and some of the others began praying out loud.

We were gradually losing speed, when we at last spotted a dim light in the distance. As we got nearer the light, we could see there were several dimmer lights around the brighter one. It looked like it might be coming from one large building, perhaps a huge rice warehouse. Meanwhile, we continued losing power. We were now about a half mile from the lighted building and moving at only ten miles per hour when we heard a sound that struck terror in our hearts. The low rumbling sound in the distance behind us gradually grew louder. I frantically nursed the accelerator pedal, fearing that it was going to cut out altogether, while the sound of several motorcycles was getting louder. Now, the engine was cutting out so much, the van was just jerking along at only four or five miles per hour!

Just as we came within fifty yards of the compound's entrance, a small, seemingly empty guard house and a bar gate blocking the entrance came into view. *Now what?* my mind raced. The loud roar and swiftly approaching headlights of the motorcycles were now bearing down on us. We had only a few yards to go to reach the closed gate. Just then, an armed guard came out of the guard house, saw our plight, and swung the gate wide open. The van jerked forward and in through the gate. Barely inside, the engine gave out a final sputter and died. Quickly, the guard swung the gate closed, just as the motorcycles rumbled up. In the light coming from the building, we could see at least four roving bandits just on the other side of the gate from us. Then, without stopping, they circled around and sped away into the darkness.

Breathing sighs of relief, some of us began crying, some started laughing; but *all* of us eventually joined in chorus saying to the guard who "just happened to be there" when we pulled up, "Thank you, thank you, thank you!"

How was it that our failing engine kept us going until we were just barely inside the gate, while at the same time, our pursuers lagged behind, just long enough for us to escape?

CHAPTER 18

WAKE UP! THE LORD IS NEAR!

Lakeland, Florida 1980 and Bangkok 1982

Beyond our everyday routines and challenges we can detect the mysterious influence of the divine: 'meaningful coincidences' that seem to be sending us messages and leading us in a particular direction."

—James Redfield

I didn't know it at the time, but the first in a chain of events that would change the course of our lives happened one Sunday morning at St. David's Episcopal Church in Lakeland, Florida where our family had been attending for the past three years. It started when Father Littleford, our interim priest, a tall, elderly gentleman whom one might have mistaken for Moses, approached me after the service and said, "David, don't you feel the Lord calling you to Holy Orders?"

His question caught me completely off guard, mainly because, not having been an Episcopalian very long, I was not familiar with the ecclesiastical lingo, and was not exactly sure what "Holy Orders" was. Not wanting to appear stupid, and guessing that it must have something very special to do with the church, I ventured a firm, "No, I have not." He didn't pursue the matter, but just smiled and turned away.

A few Sundays later, after the morning service, the ninety-something-year-old "saint" of St. David's, a woman named Elsie Gerrard, the widow of a priest, walked up to me with a paper bag in her hand. Elsie had the face of an angel, and her sky blue eyes sparkled as she approached. With a sweet smile on her face, she handed me the bag and said, "Here, David, I want you to have this."

Surprised and wondering what might be in the bag, I jokingly said to her, "Is this my brown bag lunch? What is it?"

She grinned and said, "Open it."

I reached into the bag and pulled out a beautiful priest's stole. Then I looked into the bag and saw there were several more stoles, each one a different color. Her face then took on a more serious demeanor, "These were my husband's, and I want you to have them."

Dumbfounded, and not having a clue why she was giving them to me, I thanked her, wondering, "Why me?" She accepted my thanks and without another word, she turned and was on her way.

Several weeks later, while preparing to leave for Thailand on a two-year assignment to work with refugees, Father Littleford approached me again saying, "David, don't you feel the Lord calling you to Holy Orders?"

I was puzzled at his persistence and simply replied, "No, I feel the Lord calling us to Thailand." He smiled and said no more about it. And, frankly, I thought no more about it.

Twenty months later, Karen and I were seated in a Bangkok restaurant at a large round table with several of our refugee workers who had come in from the border camps for a few days of rest and recuperation. Claire, one of our young Australian workers, was seated opposite me. During the course of conversation about how things were going in the camps, I noticed Claire peering at me quizzically from across the table. Then, with a matter-of-fact look on her face, said, "David, you look like a priest."

That being the farthest thing from my mind, I just laughed and nothing more was said about it; however, during the days that followed, Claire's words continued to resurface in my mind, almost to the point of haunting me.

I finally realized that the thought of becoming a priest had begun to infiltrate my thinking. It was beginning to follow me around like a little puppy dog. But still, the thought of the priesthood seemed kind of ridiculous. For me, it just didn't seem like a serious option. Nevertheless, soon after Claire's remark, I decided to talk with Karen about it.

She listened intently, as I explained what had been going on in my mind. I searched her face for any negative reaction, but found none. Together, we remembered the strange question Father Littleford had posed to me twice before we left for Thailand and Elsie's unexplained gift of the priest's stoles.

"Maybe they knew something you didn't," Karen suggested. "Why don't you go talk to Father Smith?"

The Reverend Bill Smith was an Anglican priest working as an editor for the United Nations in Bangkok and also serving as the interim priest at Christ Church, where we attended in Bangkok.

After listening to my story, he asked, "Well, David, do you feel like you *are* being called to prepare for the priesthood?"

"I don't know. I just feel that I would have to be absolutely sure before taking that step."

We talked for a few more minutes, until finally he said, "Well, I would suggest you just continue to make it a matter of prayer."

I left his office feeling like I was pursuing the matter as I should, but still not any more convinced that preparing for the priesthood was something I was being called to do.

When I got home, Karen agreed that I ought to just keep praying about it. "You will know," she said, "if and when you are being called."

Days went by, and thoughts about the priesthood continued to occupy my mind. I questioned myself, *Why would I want to become a priest?* The only answer that ever came was, *So that I would be nearer to the Lord.* However, I thought, *That is not a good reason to become a priest.* It even bordered on the ridiculous; one should not enter the priesthood just because he wants to be nearer the Lord. At least that's what I believed, at the time.

It was nearly midnight on a Saturday night, not long after I'd started praying about the priesthood. As I lay in bed listening to the soft rhythm of Karen's breathing, I was wide-eyed and sleepless. In an effort to join her in slumber, I decided to try something I had never done before. Instead of counting sheep to put myself to sleep, I began repeating a mantra I had learned: *"Lord, be near...Lord, be near...Lord, be near."* I went to sleep, gently breathing the words, *"Lord, be near."*

We had a radio alarm clock that we kept set to the local BBC station, which awakened us every morning. That Sunday morning, we were stirred out of a sound sleep with the rousing words of a British commentator calling out: *"Wake up! The Lord is near!"*

In that moment, I knew the words to be true—there was no doubt in my mind that God's presence surrounded me...but I was *still* not convinced I was being called to prepare for Holy Orders. All I knew, in those waking moments, was that *the Lord was near.*

CHAPTER 19

HOLY ORDERS

Thailand 1982

"At synchronous moments, you get a peek at just how connected your life is, how completely woven into the infinite tapestry of existence."

—Deepak Chopra

A Thai holiday was coming up, and we had made arrangements to go to the family equestrian camp at River Kwai located in northwestern Thailand, near the famous World War II Bridge. We had been there before, and it had become a favorite place for Karen and me to go for rest and recuperation. The girls loved it, mainly for the horseback riding.

While I was still not convinced I had a calling to the priesthood, my thoughts about pursuing Holy Orders intensified. Day and night, on the job and at home, the idea of going to seminary dominated my thinking.

Shortly before leaving for the camp, I said to Karen, "The feeling I have about going to seminary has gotten so strong, I think that somehow, during this weekend, I'm going to get an answer."

The campground was a welcome sight, and it didn't take long to unpack and settle into Porky Dorm, where we had stayed on previous visits. Porky Dorm was a rustic building with several cots and a primitive bathroom at the far end. It was built over a concrete slab, which was all that was left of an old pig sty that had been in operation many years before. It had three-foot-high cement block walls with wide mesh wire screening above them, which met a metal roof that gave off a wonderfully soothing sound in the frequent tropical rainstorms. Set amid flowering trees, bamboo thickets, and sugar cane fields, the camp was a welcome respite from our frantic pace in Bangkok. I drew in a deep breath, taking in the freshness and beauty all around.

I opened my eyes early that Sunday morning, and Porky Dorm was abuzz with the hushed voices of children and their parents talking about horses and hikes, and all the things they were going to do that day. Monday was a Thai holiday and the thought of being there in camp another day sent a surge of joy through my heart. The aroma of scrambled eggs and sausage wafted in from the nearby open-air dining hall.

After breakfast, the girls were off to the stables for riding lessons.

"I think I'll head back to Porky Dorm," I told Karen. "I feel the bunk beckoning me."

"That's fine," Karen replied, "There's a trail I haven't walked before calling me. I'll see you at lunch."

I lay down on my back and felt a peacefulness wash over me. Closing my eyes, all the world began to fade, except for the songs of birds in the surrounding trees and the faint sounds of children's voices in the distance. Sleep overtook me. Then suddenly, I was wide awake, sitting up. I reached for my Bible, which was on the stand next to my bunk. In my hand, it fell open to the Psalms, and my eyes went straight to the words of Psalm 65, verse 4: *"Blessed is he whom thou dost choose and bring near, to dwell in thy courts! We shall be satisfied with the goodness of thy house, thy holy temple!"*

Suddenly I knew! How I knew, I didn't know...I just knew. There was no longer a question in my mind.

Joy, like I had never felt before, filled my whole being, and then a deep feeling of peace. The nagging question was replaced with a calm knowing.

But what to do now? I had no idea. Then I thought, *"I'll write to Father Littleford and ask him what I need to do."* I grabbed a notebook and headed out the door, looking for a place where I could be sure to be alone. I walked to a heavily wooded area and found a log, where I sat down and wrote my Moses-like mentor a long letter. I explained everything that had happened over the past several weeks and what I was feeling at the moment. A sense of peaceful bliss swept through me again, as I closed the notebook and headed back to Porky Dorm.

It was nearly noon, and Karen and I had agreed to meet in the dining hall for lunch. I could hardly wait to tell her what had happened.

As I walked toward the dining hall, I could see Karen sitting there waiting for me. The huge smile on my face announced to her the news before I was even able to get the words out of my mouth. When I told her what had just happened, a big grin spread across her face. She said, *"I know...because I had the same feeling."*

Back in the office Tuesday morning, I handed my handwritten letter to Winnie, our Chinese secretary. "Please type this up for my signature. I'd like to get it in the mail today."

Walking into my office, I found a stack of mail on my desk. I quickly sorted through it and there, in the middle of the stack, was a letter from Father Littleford. I had not heard from him for several months. I tore open the envelope and began reading.

He asked about our family and told about some things he was doing and about the church, and then came the next sentence, *"David, don't you feel the Lord calling you to Holy Orders?"*

Up to that time, I hadn't felt the need for any more confirmations regarding a calling, but there it was anyway. I laid the letter down on my desk, wondering how the timing of it all could have been so perfect.

After a week, I began anxiously looking for a letter back from Father Littleford. Finally, after two weeks, I received the letter I had been waiting for. He said he had talked to the bishop, and the bishop had suggested I remain in Thailand another year, in order to give them time to raise the funds needed for me to start seminary.

"I can't do that," I told Karen. "Our contract is up in three months, and Food for the Hungry has already decided how they are going to reorganize after our departure."

"What to do, then?" she said. "What shall we do?"

I happened to be good friends with the Thai director of World Concern International, another relief and development agency. So I called him and told him what was going on.

"The head of World Concern from our Seattle office is coming out here next week," he said, "and we have projects in several different countries around the world. Maybe he could use you for a year somewhere."

A week later, Karen and I sat down with the head of World Concern. After listening to our story, he said, "We have a medical team working with refugees in two camps in Somalia, and we just lost our director. We need someone like you to head up our project there for the next two years. Are you interested?"

"I really don't know anything about medical programs," I said.

"You don't have to. This is an administrative position."

I looked at him hopefully, "We can give you one year."

Three months later, we were packed and on our way to Somalia—with thoughts of attending seminary dancing in my head.

CHAPTER 20

SOMALI LADY

Mogadishu, Somalia 1983

"... we are here on assignment, and the synchronicity we can live
guides us toward the accomplishment of our mission."

—James Redfield

It was the typical 100-degree-plus Somali morning. Sitting at my desk in Mogadishu, I had already worked up a sweat just pushing my pen, when Ali, my Somali assistant, a clean shaven man in his mid-thirties, walked in. The expression on his face told me there was a problem.

"What's the matter, Ali?"

"My niece was in a bus when it crashed and she broke her arm, really bad."

"How badly?"

"You can see the bone poking out. It happened a few days ago and she is in very much pain now."

"Where is she?"

"At her home on the other side of Mogadishu."

I grabbed my keys. "Let's go."

Out the front door we were hit by the scorching sun. I nodded to Abdi, our guard, a little guy who was a good four inches shorter than the average Somali man. I could always find him in a shaded area next to the Land Cruiser inside the locked gate. His job was to guard the gate and watch for intruders, including monkeys, who occasionally slipped over the wall surrounding the house and office. I knew Abdi to be faithful in at least two areas of life: in the saying of his prayers at the hours assigned for all Muslims to pray throughout the day (including touching his forehead down to his prayer carpet), and being prompt opening the gate for our comings and goings, except for those times when he was praying. (Those were the times that taught me patience.)

Dust from the rutted dirt road curled up behind us, as we headed across town. As we approached Ali's neighborhood—an area where small, square dwellings were crammed close together—the road narrowed. The rickety, little white houses all had shutters and no window panes. We slowed down. Small children were everywhere along the roadside playing with sticks and homemade toys. Several older boys were in the road, kicking a little ball made of banana fiber in a game that looked like soccer, while adults sat in small groups in the scant shade provided by the buildings.

"There," Ali said, pointing ahead toward one of the houses, the front door of which was open. A handful of children stopped what they were doing and gazed at us as we pulled up in front of the house and parked. Ali walked to the front door and called out a greeting. When he heard a response from inside, he motioned for me to enter with him.

Three women surrounded a bed in the middle of the front room. In the bed, with her left arm propped up on a pillow, was a pretty young woman who appeared to be about nineteen.

Ali walked over to the bed, and leaning over whispered something to the young woman. She whispered back adding a pained smile.

Her arm was heavily bandaged. I asked Ali, "Did you

see her arm when the bandage was not on?"

"Yes. The bone in her arm is completely broken, and the wound was oozing."

I immediately thought of the possibility of gangrene. "We need to get her to the hospital, Ali."

He said something to the women, and they immediately gathered around the young woman. Very gently, they began moving her off the bed and onto her feet. She let out a muffled cry and her face showed she was in excruciating pain. Two of the women carefully assisted her as she began shuffling forward. The other woman carried the pillow supporting her arm. They walked her slowly out the door and to the Land Cruiser, taking several minutes to maneuver her into the back seat. Ali joined me in the front.

"Where is the hospital from here?" I asked Ali.

"Somewhere in that direction," he said, pointing, "I've never been there."

I drove slowly, trying to avoid the worst bumps. Eventually we reached a hard-top road that had a minimum of potholes. As I drove along, not knowing for sure if we were even going in the right direction, I noticed, in my rear view mirror, a little white Fiat following behind us. I slowed down, hoping to get a look at the occupants, thinking that perhaps they could give us directions. Finally they were close enough, so I could see what appeared to be two Catholic nuns in their traditional habits. I slowed down, while at the same time, I waved my arm out the window for them to stop behind me, which they did.

I opened my door, jumped out, and ran back to their car. Their window was down and I asked, "Can you tell me where the hospital is?"

They looked at each other, then the one driving spoke up with a heavy Italian accent, "Follow us."

We stayed close behind the nuns' car, until we could

see, off to the right, a large, old rambling building that I figured must be the hospital. We proceeded to follow them, until we reached a road that led down to the hospital. There, the nuns slowed down and pointed the way. I waved a thank you, as the nuns disappeared around a bend.

The archaic building was huge and obviously left over from colonial days. In fact, one got the feeling that nothing had been done to the building since the colonists left.

As we pulled up to the front of the hospital, I asked Ali to tell the women to wait in the car with his niece until we could find out how we might get her admitted. I had no idea at the time how impossible it would be to get her in to see a doctor or even a nurse. I signaled Ali and he followed me up the walkway toward the front door. My thought was to have Ali try to convince the receiving nurse to at least get someone to look at his niece. As I pushed the door open, I was nearly knocked over by a man hurrying out. Much to my surprise, I heard my name. "Hello! David!"

It was the Egyptian doctor I had often seen in church. I had asked him one time, several weeks earlier where he practiced, and he'd said he was on the road most of the time. Naturally, I was surprised to see him there.

I quickly explained the situation to him, including all I could about the young woman's condition.

He listened intently, then said, "Let me see her."

We walked him out to the Land Cruiser and I asked Ali to explain to the doctor what had happened to her arm and when it was broken.

He looked carefully at her bandaged arm, then said, "Follow me."

The women slowly and carefully maneuvered her out and began the long walk to the front door. We followed the doctor through an empty area that looked like it had once been a lobby—one that had seen better days—then up some stairs and down a long corridor. Walking slowly, I could see, in each room we passed, six to eight patients lying on the floor on mats. Some had people in civilian clothes tending to them—family, I supposed—feeding them and helping them to drink. I asked the doctor about the patients' care.

"Oh, there are very few nurses here and hardly any doctors. The conditions are so very poor here it is difficult to get medical people to come. And medicines are scarce, as well. Families who bring patients here end up giving most of the care."

His reply was sobering, actually depressing. I swallowed hard as I could readily see the conditions he described surrounding me.

We continued walking to what looked like the far end of the hospital where there was a long flight of stairs leading down to a large secluded room. I got the distinct feeling we had arrived at an exclusive part of the hospital where only select patients were treated, perhaps just top government officials and their families.

From the door, I could see several men and women in white gowns. We waited, as my doctor friend went in and spoke to one of the men. The man turned and looked at us, then said something to two young aides who came to the door and escorted Ali's niece inside, while our doctor friend came back to us and announced, "They'll take care of her."

I felt a huge sense of relief as we climbed back up the stairs. Considering how long the wound had been festering and the condition she was in, I had little hope they would be able to save her arm. My hope was that they could at least save her life.

Every day I checked with Ali to see how she was doing. Then one day he came in with a huge smile on his face and said, "She's home, and her arm is going to be okay."

I often think about Ali's niece, and wonder where she might be today. She probably got married and raised some little ones of her own, and was no doubt thankful she had *both* arms to cuddle them.

Then I think about the nuns in their little white Fiat and how they pointed the way to the hospital. And I think about how I arrived at the hospital entrance at the precise moment to bump into my Egyptian doctor friend.

And I wonder, was that all just a coincidence?

I don't think so.

CHAPTER 21

BOMBING HALBA

Halba Refugee Camp, Lugh, Somalia 1983
"Synchronicity indicates that the timing of events is tied into an unseen pattern of connections."

—David Richo

The heat of a new day was already blowing in through the open window of our office at 7:59 a.m.as I sat facing the radio receiver that connected us with our medical team at Halba. One minute later, through the crackles and pops of the receiver, the voice of our team leader, Norm, came through loud and clear, though more intense than usual.

"Ootje and Dharma's cottage was bombed last night...but thankfully, they were both away. Ootje's in Mogadishu attending a medical meeting, and Dharma's back home on sick leave."

"Was anyone hurt?" I asked.

"No one was hurt. But it could have been a *lot* worse."

"How's that?"

"There were two blasts, approximately four minutes apart. The first hit around 2:00 a.m. and got everybody out of their cabins to see what was happening. I'm grateful to say, though, that no one had gotten close enough to the bomb site, so when the second blast went off, nobody was hurt. I think we were all in a state of shock"

"What's left of the cottage?"

"It's completely destroyed."

"I'm coming up," I said. "There'll have to be an investigation. I'll see you when I get there. Anything else?"

"That's it."

Turning off the radio, I picked up the phone and called Howell Sasser, an officer friend attached to the U.S. Army unit stationed in Mogadishu.

"Hello, Howie. This is David. One of our nurses' cottages at Halba got bombed last night, and I'll be heading up there today. Can you come along?"

Howie hesitated, but then said, "I can leave in an hour."

"I'll pick you up."

The road leading out of Mogadishu toward the two Halba refugee camps was blacktop for the first several miles, then after that it was mostly dirt and sand. The camps were spread out over several square miles close to the Ethiopian border, a 240-mile trek westward across the desert from Mogadishu. The refugees, about 40,000 all together, are ethnic Somalis who had lived for generations in the eastern part of Ethiopia that traditionally was part of Somaliland; but after the Soviets took over Ethiopia, Cuban soldiers, who the Soviets brought over to fight for them, chased them back across the Somali border at gunpoint.

It was 3:00 p.m. and blistering hot when Howie and I arrived at the medical team compound, which was located just outside one of the desert camps. The cottages housing the team formed a huge semi-circle under the few trees that had been left standing. Norm walked us

96

around the site that had been reduced to shattered bits and pieces of wood and rubble. Pointing at a twisted piece of metal lying about 40 feet from the blasts, he said, "That's part of what's left of Ootje's or Dharma's bed. I hate to imagine what this scene would look like if either of our two nurses had been here last night."

"These were obviously time bombs," Howie said, "and set about four minutes apart. Whoever the bomber was, he or she was obviously thinking that after four minutes, the other refugee workers would be drawn in close enough to the scene of the first blast, so that the second bomb would get them. This was an act of sheer terrorism." Howie paused, looked around grimly, then added, "There *will* be an investigation."

After we looked over the remains of the cottage, I called a team meeting and discussed, among other things, what the bomber's purpose might have been and what the chances might be of a repeat performance.

"Somebody obviously doesn't want us to be here," one of the nurses pitched in.

We talked at length about the safety issue and the likelihood of getting additional security.

That night, I lay in bed pondering—"How was it that both nurses were away on the night of the blast, when normally at least one of them is always there?" And— "What was it that held all our team members back far enough from the second blast, that none of them was hurt?"

I finally drifted off to sleep whispering thanks for the dedicated lives of our nurses, and for their safety.

CHAPTER 22

THE SOMALI BOX

Mogadishu, Somalia - Sewanee, Tennessee 1983

"Something beyond all of us is guiding the change we are passing through, and we have no choice or say in that. Our only responsibility is to surrender, and to allow that to do its work."

—Barbara Marx Hubbard

"Did you say there are *no* ships coming into the Mogadishu port that will be going on to the U. S.?" I stared at the CARE official in disbelief.

"Then how in the world am I going to get our belongings back home?" My CARE friend shrugged, giving me a sympathetic smile. Speechless, I turned and headed back to my vehicle, wondering exactly how I was going to break the bad news to Karen.

"You mean we're going to have to *leave* our belongings *here*? I can't believe it!" she moaned. "And we had that big wooden box that's sitting out front built for *nothing*!"

"What can we do?" I returned. "Maybe my CARE friend was wrong, and there *will* be a ship coming into port that could carry our belongings back to a U. S. port...*any* port. When Ali comes in tomorrow, I'm going to ask him to go check with the port authority, just to make sure."

The next morning, Ali came back from the port authority with the bad news. "It's true, David. There's no ship coming here that will be going to the U. S."

"We fly out in four weeks," Karen said, "so I guess we better start sorting out those few things we need to keep...and just leave everything else here...for whoever." There was a clear note of sorrow and regret in her voice.

One week before we were scheduled to fly out, Abdi came running in to the office and announced, "David, I just checked back with the port authority again, and they said that an American cargo ship is docked here *right now*, and it can take your box, *if* we get all the paperwork signed and your box down to the dock by tomorrow before the ship leaves at 11:00 a.m."

A mad scramble began immediately with the resorting of everything we had brought with us a year earlier, plus the few things we had purchased in Somalia. Meanwhile, Abdi got the paperwork process started at the government offices. He warned me that we were required to get signatures from *several different officials* in order to have anything shipped out of the country.

At 9:15 a.m. the next morning, I was scouring the house for nails to seal the lid down on the box. Not able to find even one, and realizing it was too late to try and find nails in the market, I desperately started pulling nails out of furniture, door frames, and everything in sight that had been nailed to anything else. Abdi had already made arrangements for a truck to pick up the box and take it down to the dock, which was only about two miles away.

At 9:40, when I pounded the last crooked, rusty nail into the lid of the box, Abdi had still not returned with the signed papers, plus the truck had not arrived. However, at 10:20, Abdi came skidding in. "Get all the signatures?" I asked.

"Yes! The truck's not here?"

Nervously I glanced at my watch. "Not yet," I said.

Just then, we heard the roar of a truck engine coming

down our rutted, dusty street. Within minutes, we had the box loaded up and were on our way, following closely behind the truck.

"Thank God!" I yelled, as we turned a corner and saw the ship was still tied up at the dock. We followed the truck through a gate and onto the dock, where the driver pulled up beside the ship. When I got out, I could smell the diesel and hear the low rumble of the ship's engine. We watched as our box was unloaded from the truck onto the dock no more than ten yards from the ship, which was obviously ready to set sail. Several men from inside the ship took heavy ropes and tied them around the box, as the ship's giant boom moved slowly over to where it was positioned directly above the box. Before we knew it, the box was swinging in the air, then lowered steadily, and gently set on the deck of the ship.

"Phew! Can you believe it?" I said to Karen.

In less than three minutes after our box touched down on the deck, the lines holding the ship to the dock were thrown off, and the ship, with all the possessions that had sustained us over the past year, was on its way back to America.

We stood there speechless, watching the ship make its way slowly out to sea. Still in disbelief that it had all come together in just the last twenty-four hours, we drove to a spot a couple miles up the coast, where we had a perfect view of the ship heading out to the deep waters of the Indian Ocean. Karen and I stood on the beach watching, as the old cargo ship gradually sank deeper and deeper into the horizon until all that was left was a speck in the distance.

As we drove back to the house, I fought off fears about how our precious box could ever make it safely all the way around the Horn of Africa and across the Atlantic to an American port, after who knows how many port stops along the way.

Just then, Karen interrupted my thoughts. "Are you sure our new address, School of Theology, University of the South, Sewanee, Tennessee, was on all the paperwork?"

I smiled. "Yes, Ali took care of that. When we get back to the States, I'll ask John to put a tracer on the box and make sure it gets delivered to us from the port where the ship docks.

Six weeks later, after visits with family and friends in Florida, Karen, the girls, and I arrived in Sewanee, where we were put up for the night in a college guest house. The next morning, while we were having breakfast, a woman from the seminary housing office approached our table. She introduced herself, and then asked, "Well, would you like to go see where you'll be living?"

Our chorus of five answered an enthusiastic, "Yes!"

We all piled into her car, and off we went to see the house where we would be living for many months to follow. Cutting across the beautiful forested, mountaintop campus, the car slowed, as we approached a little stone house. Then, before we even stopped, the girls started screaming. "Our box! Our box!"

The driver smiled, "Oh yes, your box arrived just *yesterday*, about the *same time* you got here."

I shook my head in wonderment.
"*Timing*," I mused, "*timing*."

CHAPTER 23

"DAVID!"

Atlanta 1984

"As you consciously poise yourself in the realization that you live in pure Spirit, new power will be born within you. You will find yourself renewed by the Divine Life, led by Divine Intelligence, and guarded by the Divine Love."

—Ernest Holmes

Those of us who survived the first year of seminary found ourselves out doing field work the following summer. For me, it was at Georgia Mental Health Institute in Atlanta, working as an assistant chaplain with alcoholics and drug addicts mornings and with teens suffering from mental illnesses in the afternoons and evenings. I had been graciously invited by some old friends from our days in Nashville together, Dr. Dixie and Fran Snider, to stay the summer with their family in Tucker, a suburb of Atlanta. Dixie was the Chief Science Officer with the Centers for Disease Control and Prevention.

It all began early one morning, when I awoke an hour earlier than usual. I had apparently set my alarm clock an hour early by mistake and didn't realize it until I went out into the kitchen and looked at the clock there. The house was unusually quiet. Everyone else was still in bed or off to work. I went back to my room and decided to catch another couple of winks, so I reset my alarm and lay down on the bed. I began to doze. The next thing I knew, I heard someone call my name. "DAVID!"

I sat straight up in bed and turned toward the closed door, wondering who might be calling me. I first thought of their daughter, Ann. No...it wasn't her voice. Fran? Dixie? No...no, it wasn't either of their voices. It was a crystal-clear voice that called my name.

I got up and walked to the door, opened it and looked out into the hallway. Early morning light was just beginning to chase away the dark of the night. All was still.

Perplexed, I went back and sat on the edge of the bed, thinking, What in the world is going on? I did hear someone call my name...quite clearly, in fact.

I closed my eyes and let my mind wander back to our days in Thailand. I thought of Adelia, who had joined our team as a volunteer and how she used to travel with us to the refugee camps on the Thai-Cambodian border. She was a deeply spiritual person and a devout Catholic, besides being a dear friend of our family. I thought about what she had told me one time, about what she would do when she felt there was a message out there for her, but didn't quite understand what it was. She told me how she would close her eyes and go into a deeply quiet, meditative state, and pretty soon see in her mind's eye the reference to a scripture. She would then get her Bible and look up the scripture.

When she said that, as much as I respected her, I was skeptical; but I never forgot what she said.

I sat there wondering how and why I had heard my name called, and if there might be a message for me. Then I thought, Why not try and do what Adelia did? I mean, why not?

I repositioned myself on the bed, and got

comfortable, with my back against the headboard, and closed my eyes. In silence, I tried releasing all my thoughts, to get myself into a quiet, meditative state. Finally, I felt like I didn't have to try any more, and there was just a peaceful silence within me. After about a minute I saw in my mind's eye, a scriptural reference that looked like I Corinthians 3:17.

Having no idea what I Corinthians 3:17 might say, I jumped to my feet and grabbed my Bible. I read verse 17, then verses 16 and 17 together:

Do you not know that you are God's temple, and that God's Spirit dwells in you. If anyone destroys God's temple, God will destroy him. For God's temple is holy, and that temple you are.

Stunned, I wondered, What am I doing that's destroying my body? I'm not smoking. What am I eating or drinking that might be hurting me?

I was puzzled, because I believed this was definitely a message that must have some significance for me. I decided to memorize the verses, thinking that the meaning might become clear later.

I got dressed, fixed myself some breakfast, and drove to the addiction center, continuing to wonder how those verses might relate to me. The morning was uneventful, and soon it was time for lunch. Every day at lunchtime, three or four of us seminarians would walk over to the Georgia Mental Health Institute cafeteria and have lunch together; but that particular day, every one of my friends took off in a different direction. So, I walked to the cafeteria by myself and took my place at the end of the long line of hungry people.

Less than a minute later, a young man walked up behind me and joined the line. I recognized him as one of the addicts from our group, and recalled his name was David. We greeted each other, and he immediately began telling me all about his guitar and the band he played in. He continued talking nonstop, until we reached the place where we picked up our food. After paying the cashier, I turned and asked him if he would like to share a table. As we were getting seated, he continued to talk about his experiences with the band.

Finally there was a pause in his monologue, and I said, "I'd like to tell you about a strange experience I had this morning." I told him how I had been dozing on my bed when I heard a voice call my name: "David!" And then I told him everything that happened after that, and when I got to the end, I quoted the scripture that I had memorized.

Suddenly, David's mouth dropped open, and he went silent. Finally he said, "That...was for me."

His voice took on a totally different tone when he added, "This morning, when I got up, I was extremely depressed. I went out to the kitchen, and walked over to the drawer where I keep a butcher knife. I reached into the drawer, picked up the knife, and I was just about to kill myself...when something stopped me."

Then he paused, and added, "The words you read this morning...were meant for me."

That evening, as I lay in bed, I thought about Adelia, and the things she used to tell us about experiences she'd had, which seemed to me to be completely out of the realm of reality, at least of reality as I knew it. Then I thought about my own experience, and David's reaction when I told him about it. And I thought about other experiences I'd had that were also out of the realm of our normal, everyday reality. I pondered those thoughts, wondering about this unseen reality that seems to be at work in the universe, a reality that seems to be watching out for our good, guiding us and protecting us. I continued reflecting, until sleep finally claimed its own.

CHAPTER 24

FIRE IN THE BUS

Tullahoma, Tennessee 1985

"When we begin to think more about the interdependence of things, we take our place as one more star in the magnificent universe, rather than as the sun around which the universe revolves."

—Joan Borysenko

How many times must it take to learn that a helping hand is not always helpful? It was Friday evening and Karen, the girls, and I were on our way to Tullahoma in "Brown Bear," our old Volkswagen pop-top bus, for our regular Friday evening out for supper and shopping. After a long week of seminary studies for me, work for the dean of the seminary for Karen, and school for the girls, the whole family looked forward to this weekly outing.

On the outskirts of town, we stopped at a Shell station for gas. One of the men on duty came out and asked, "Want me to check your oil?"

"Yes, please," I replied.

I followed the man around to the back of the bus and watched as he opened the rear engine cover door, reached in and pulled out the oil stick. He held the stick for nearly a full minute, up close to his squinting eyes, and then gently placed it back. "Oil's okay, Sir, but ya' see them two wires a'hangin' there?" he asked pointing at the engine.

"Yes, I do. I have wondered about those wires."

"They somehow got pulled apart. I don't think they's supposed to be a'danglin' there like that. Ya' want me ta' reattach 'em?"

"I think that would probably be a good idea, don't you think?"

I watched as he attached the two wires, and wondered how the old bus had operated so well with the wires separated like they were.

"Thank you, Sir. I appreciate your checking everything out," I said, as he closed the engine door.

He smiled a sweet smile, "T'was nothin', Sir," he said, as he finished pumping our gas tank full. I watched as he placed the gas cap back on, and I went inside and paid the bill.

He was still standing by the bus when I came out. "Thanks again," I said, as I climbed back into the bus, and we were off again down the highway.

I could hear the voices of the girls chattering behind me, when suddenly, Bekki, with some alarm in her voice, said, "Hey, Papa, where's that smoke coming from?" I looked back and saw smoke pouring into the rear of the bus. I immediately pulled off to the side of the highway, jumped out and ran around to the other side of the bus.

"Everybody out!" I shouted, as I slid open the side door, then ran to the back of the bus and opened the engine door. The wiring was fiery red hot and smoke was pouring out from all around the engine. I glanced around and saw we were directly in front of a liquor store with several cars parked in front. I dashed across the parking lot and into the store. Brushing past customers, I went directly to the counter where a customer was being waiting on. Breathless, I interrupted their exchange: "My VW bus's engine is on fire. Do you have a fire extinguisher?" The man disappeared quickly into the back of the store and reappeared moments later with an extinguisher that he practically threw at me. It all happened in a matter of seconds. I ran with it out the door and sprinted toward the bus. A small crowd had already begun to gather, as smoke was pouring out the back of the bus. I could feel the heat, as I peered through the smoke at what looked like an engine ready to blow up. I pulled the trigger of the extinguisher and a broad stream of white foam came spewing out, covering the entire engine.

Minutes later, as the smoke began to clear, I could see the charred engine and wires, and how very close they were to the gas tank that had just been filled, and how close it all had come to exploding.

As I walked back to the liquor store with the empty extinguisher, thoughts raced through my mind about how it *just happened* that of all the places where we *could* have stopped, we had come to a stop *directly* in front of a place where a fire extinguisher was readily available...like it was there *just waiting* for me to pick it up. In my heart though, I *knew* it was *not just by chance* that we had come to an abrupt stop exactly where we did.

CHAPTER 25

A SMILE IN THE SKY

Tracy City, Tennessee 1987

"This Presence, warm, personal, and colorful, responds to me. It is within, around, and through me and embraces all things. Today, I accept my partnership with the Infinite."

—Ernest Holmes

Saying goodbye to seminary classmates was bittersweet, mostly sweet—friendly hugs and well-wishes galore; term papers, exams, and practice sermons now a thing of the past.

After graduation and serving one year as a deacon, I was more than ready to join the ranks of the priesthood; not that I believed it would make me any holier, but I felt ordination would give me an authentic voice to express the teachings of the faith as I understood them.

It was one of those late afternoon spring showers that sneak up seemingly out of nowhere and, unfortunately, I had left the windows down in Brown Bear, our VW bus. We had been so busy packing up the house in Sewanee, where we had lived the last four years, I had forgotten to roll them up. The interior was soaked! This was the day of my ordination, which was to take place in Christ Church in Tracy City, a small coal mining town that had seen its day nearly a century before. Now, with most of the mines closed, this little town that lay just twelve miles northeast of Sewanee was suffering from a staggeringly high unemployment rate and all the concomitant problems. The county was one of the poorest in the state and known for its high crime rate and drug problems. One could actually see the sense of despair on the faces of many in the community.

Clouds were still lingering overhead, as I drove a still-drying Brown Bear to church, where I was to meet Bishop Reynolds early, so we could look over the service together. I was more than a little nervous about meeting the Bishop, and it didn't help matters when he pointed out the fact that the rear end of my trousers was wet from leaving my window down. He asked about Karen and the girls, and I told him they would be arriving shortly with one of our daughters' girlfriends, and that all four girls would be serving as acolytes. Little did I know that this ultra-traditional little church had *never,* in its 127-year history, had even one single *female* acolyte.

All in our finest vestments, the processional party gathered at the back of the church: the four young acolytes, choir, gospeler, verger, myself, and, lastly, the Bishop bringing up the rear.

It was not until the organ began thundering out the processional hymn that I noticed that all four of my young female acolytes were *barefoot.* I was sure this would only add to the shock felt by several of the elder members, who witnessed, for the first time, not only acolytes of the *"other gender"* but no less barefoot, parading merrily up the aisle, leading the procession in.

The service went without a hitch, though. I was prayed over by the Bishop, which by tradition, moved me up a notch on the ecclesiastical ladder, from deacon to priest. I don't, however, remember feeling any sacred milestone being passed.

During the reception in the parish hall, while the offended elders, with their little cups of fruit punch and dainty finger foods in hand, fluttered around over the issue of the gender *and* the bare feet, Bobby Foster, the church treasurer and town undertaker approached me and said, "David, during the service I went out into the parking lot to check on the cars and, when I turned to come back, I looked up...and *directly over the church, there was a beautiful rainbow.*"

That night, after everyone had departed and Karen and I were back in the sanctuary of our home discussing how the young barefoot acolytes must have upset some of the elders, I told her what Bobby had said about the rainbow.

Karen smiled, "Yeah, there'll always be some glowering, but you can bet that rainbow in the sky was nothing less than God smiling."

CHAPTER 26

BIRDS 'N GIRLS

Tracy City and Sewanee, Tennessee and Berea, Kentucky 1988
"...the whole universe, despite its immensity and solidity, is a projection of God's nature. Those astonishing events we call miracles give us clues to the workings of this ineffable intelligence."

—Deepak Chopra

The day had turned into one of those fabulous fall afternoons in eastern Tennessee with the sun flickering through the multicolored leaves. It was so pleasant outside, I had actually *wanted* to pick up the rake. While standing out in the front yard beside a big pile of leaves, I heard the familiar sound of our VW bug coming up the road. "Froghopper" was the name the girls had given our bright green little bug that got Tabbi back and forth to school every day.

I looked up when I heard the Froghopper's door slam, and saw Tabbi walking toward me with a huge grin on her face. As she got closer, I did a double-take. There was a bird on her left shoulder.

"Tabbi, there's a bird on your shoulder!"

Her grin broadened. "He's been on my shoulder since this morning."

"What? I don't believe it!"

As I edged forward, I could see that the dark gray, plain-looking bird didn't seem to mind my approaching.

"This morning at school during break time, I was sitting on the steps, and this bird flew down onto the steps just a few feet from me. It didn't seem to mind being close to me, so I started talking to it; and then I asked it to come to me. I held out my hand and, finally, after a lot of coaxing, it hopped a little closer. I kept talking to it very quietly, and it slowly got closer and closer...until it was *almost* to my outstretched hand. After some more coaxing, it finally hopped onto my hand; and then, gradually, it climbed up my arm and onto my shoulder."

"What did you do then?"

"Well, by that time, the bell had already rung and I was late for my English class. So I got up very slowly and walked across campus and into my classroom with the bird still on my shoulder. In the classroom, we got some weird looks...and all kinds of whistles and calls from my classmates."

"What did the teacher say?"

"She was pretty cool. She just asked me to sit down."

"Did the bird just stay perched on your shoulder?"

"Yes, and he didn't seem to care about so many people being around, either."

"I can't believe this! And has he just stayed on your shoulder all day?"

"Yes."

"Even when you got in Froghopper and drove home?"

"Yes, just like he is right now." Still grinning, she turned and walked toward the house, while the bird remained stationary on her shoulder.

Not long after she got into the house, the bird took flight to investigate all the nooks and crannies of its new habitat.

Shortly after supper, the phone rang and I answered it. It was Debbi calling from college in Berea. As we talked, I kept hearing a strange sound in the background; so finally I asked, "What's that noise I keep hearing?"

"Oh, that's a little bird," she replied.

"A *bird*? Where did you get a *bird*?"

"Well, today I was riding my bike across campus and as I was passing a bush, this bird flew out of the bush and lit on my shoulder."

I nearly dropped the phone. "And it stayed on your shoulder?"

"Yes. It just stayed on my shoulder as I rode along...and when I reached the street and went out into the traffic, it just hung on."

"It didn't mind the traffic?"
"Didn't seem to."

"And it stayed with you all the way home and into your apartment?"

"Yes, it's right here."

"Well, do I have something to tell you!"

I started to tell her about Tabbi's bird, then I stopped and handed the phone to Tabbi. "Here, *you* tell her," I said.

Karen and I listened as the two girls talked and laughed long into the night.

Later in bed, Karen and I talked about the birds, and finally I asked, "Could that *possibly* have been *just a coincidence*?"

There was a long pause...and I waited. Soon, all I heard was the gentle rhythm of her breathing.

CHAPTER 27

HOSANNA

Monteagle, Tennessee 1990-present

"Synchronicities have therefore served as the starting point on a journey that has led us to the limits of human imagination. Once we realize that our consciousness is without limit, then it becomes possible for us to engage in a creative transformation of our own lives and of the society we live in."

—F. David Peat

My intention was to meet with the Vicar, but that was interrupted when two women, one of whom I knew, came bustling out of his door.

"David Crippen, fancy meeting you here!" my friend Marilyn Williams exclaimed.

"What are you doing here?" I asked.

"Probably the same thing as you...I came to see Archie. Here, I want you to meet my friend, Catherine Brown," Marilyn said, placing a gentle hand on her friend's shoulder.

Catherine was short and trim with white hair and sparkly blue eyes.

We exchanged greetings, and then I looked at

Marilyn. "I haven't seen you since our days of protesting together over the proposed hazardous waste incinerator at New Hope. What are you doing these days?"

"Catherine and I are heading over to the convent at St. Mary's to talk with Sister Lucy, to see if they might consider giving us a piece of their land to build a home for young people like Bill, Catherine's son," she said, as she glanced over at Catherine.

"Bill is twenty-eight, has cerebral palsy, and is in a wheelchair," Catherine said. "He can't live by himself, as he needs a caregiver. I've been taking care of him for twenty-eight years, but now I have some health issues and I don't know how much longer I can keep it up. I'm afraid he's facing a nursing home. I know there are some nice nursing homes around, but they aren't made for intelligent young people like Bill, who are in their twenties."

"Yes, we're hoping the sisters at St. Mary's will give us some land," Marilyn chimed in. "Then, we would start raising money to build a home for Bill and young people like him, people whose minds are good, but whose bodies are not working for them...a place where there are caregivers doing for them what they are unable to do for themselves."

"It would be *their* home and not just an institution," Catherine added, "a place where they would live together and could *really* call 'home.'"

"Sounds like a great idea to me," I said.

"Last summer," Catherine replied, "I heard about a place in Florida that takes disabled young people like Bill. So, I called and found out that Bill could move in for two weeks, while one of the residents was home on a visit. We moved Bill in...and when the two weeks were up and I went by to pick him up, he told me he liked it so much, he would like to move in permanently. This place is called Wheelhouse, because all the residents there are in wheelchairs." Catherine didn't notice the smile appear on my face, as she went on. "So, anyway, I talked to the director, a woman named Pete, Pete Wesley, and asked her if Bill could be placed on the waiting list to get in. Pete looked at me and said, 'Catherine, so many people are trying to get in here, we don't even *have* a waiting list...and besides that, nobody's moving out. There needs to be a place like this every fifty miles up and down the highway. *You go back to Tennessee and start your own.*'"

"And *that's* what we aim to do," Marilyn said, with a determined look in her eyes.

At that point in our conversation, I could not stop grinning. I looked at Catherine and said, "Listen, I used to live in Lakeland, Florida, where Wheelhouse is located, and *I've been there*, and I *know* Pete. In fact, Pete and I are good friends. When we were living in Lakeland and attending St. David's church, the Wheelhouse people, at least five or six of them, would come rolling into church every Sunday, without fail."

I could have blown Catherine over with one poof. Her eyes shone with tears, and she just shook her head. Finally, she said, "I can't believe it!"

"Well, you have a dream...a really wonderful dream of what you're hoping to do," I said. "If Pete could do it, why couldn't you? And by the way, if you decide to organize and form a committee or something, I'd be interested. Just give me a call."

Six months later, my phone rang. "David, this is Marilyn Williams. Remember our conversation a few months ago at Holy Comforter Church?"

"Sure, I remember."

"Well, Bishop Tharp is coming here today to discuss environmental and disability issues, and I'm going to present the dream that we talked with you about...you know, about the need for a home for young people like Bill. Can you come?"

At the meeting, Marilyn laid out the need for a "home" like she and Catherine were dreaming about. A lively discussion followed; and at the end, the bishop gave

121

a thumbs up. That was all that was needed to encourage a small group—Catherine, Marilyn, Catherine's long-time friend, Molly Miles, and me—to regroup immediately after the meeting to flesh out some of the ideas that had been discussed. By the time we all had to leave, the enthusiasm was so high, we decided to meet again in two weeks at the School of Theology in Sewanee. There, we agreed that in order to keep the momentum going, we would begin meeting weekly.

During the next several months we raised enough money to make visits to similarly designed homes in Georgia, North Carolina, Pennsylvania, New Jersey, and New York—homes that we thought might serve as good models for what we were hoping to do. Meanwhile, several experienced individuals joined in to help, and a Board of Directors was formed. The Board named their newly formed organization, *Hosanna*, a name that seemed appropriate for its two meanings: a *cry for help*, and a *shout of praise*. We continued raising money, until the Board decided we had enough funds coming in to hire an executive director and a secretary, whose express purpose would be to raise enough money to purchase land and build the first completely accessible house for eight physically challenged young people, plus the necessary caregivers. The Board asked me to be the executive director and Karen the secretary, so I took a leave from the parish ministry and got started working full-time on the task of helping to make the dream come true.

Three years later, the first ten-bedroom house was completed, and Bill, along with other physically challenged young people, moved in, forming the first *Hosanna family*.

Today there are two Hosanna houses on a beautiful seven-acre piece of ground in a nice residential neighborhood in Chattanooga. Each resident has his or her own private space and each house has a large common room, dining area, and a completely accessible kitchen. Evening meals are family style, giving each family member opportunity to share their day. Like any family, they have their good times and their not-so-good times; but in the end, they never need to fear being left alone.

How often I've thought about the day I "chanced" running into those two women coming out of the Vicar's office, and the drama that began to unfold that day that ended in the building of two Hosanna houses and families. But the story did *not begin* that day. If I had not known Marilyn from meetings before, how could I have ever been introduced to Catherine and her son, Bill? And if Bill had not gone to Wheelhouse in Lakeland, and had Pete not challenged Catherine to "Go back to Tennessee and start your own," and if it had not been for Bill...and his cerebral palsy...So where *did* the story begin?

CHAPTER 28

ROAD ANGEL

New Jersey 1991

"These days, however, when we think of synchronicity in spiritual terms, we are usually observing a depth of multiple, unfolding interactions that are concurrently coming forth, almost as if by some special programming that is unknown to us."

—Margaret Stortz

We were somewhere in western New Jersey. I was driving and Marilyn, without benefit of a GPS, was our navigator. She was in the front seat, totally absorbed with the New Jersey map spread out on her lap. Catherine and Molly were in the back. Marilyn had been in touch with three organizations in New York and New Jersey that ran homes for young people with disabilities, homes that we thought might be good models for us to look at.

"How are we doing?" I asked, glancing over at Marilyn.

"I know where we're going, but I don't know exactly where we are."

"Does that mean we're lost?" Molly piped up from the back.

"Well, I think we're going the wrong way, right now."

That woke up Catherine. "Well then, let's turn

around."

"I see where we need to go," Marilyn said, pointing to a spot on the map.

"Yes, but where are *we*?" Molly insisted.

I glanced over at Marilyn. "I think we need to turn around," she said.

I could see an exit coming up, but there was no sign indicating where we were. I took the exit and turned left at the top of the ramp to cross over the highway. Up ahead on the other side, I noticed a man standing beside his parked car. I figured he had probably run out of gas and needed help. As we approached the man, he began waving his *arms* for us to stop. I slowed down. Then suddenly he began shouting, "You're going the wrong way! You're going the wrong way!"

"Let's keep going," Catherine said from the back.

"Yeah, let's go!" Molly said, "We don't know who this guy is." I pulled away slowly, heading back down a parallel road, wondering what in the world that was all about.

"Some crazy kook, I guess," Marilyn said. "But I wonder how he knew we were going the wrong way."

About a minute later, in my rearview mirror, I saw the same man in his car racing up behind us. Then he sped past us and disappeared around the bend up ahead. As we rounded the bend, we looked, and there he was again, this time, out in the middle of the road waving his arms for us to stop. I slowed to a stop, and the man ran around to the driver's side of our car and motioned with his hand for me to roll my window down.

"Where are you going?" he asked.

While that was a reasonable question given our circumstances, it seemed curious coming from a stranger.

Not certain exactly how to answer, I looked over at Marilyn. She told him the name of the organization we were going to visit and that it was a special kind of home for physically challenged young people. Then she added the name of the town where it was located.

The man looked concerned, then said, "I'm familiar with that town, and there's *no* such place like you mentioned *there*."

"But it *must* be there," Marilyn said, holding up an envelope in her hand, "because here's the return address on this envelope the director sent me." She handed me the envelope to show him.

He looked at the address and said, "I *know* that community, and there is *no* organization like you describe *there*. That's an upscale bedroom community with a golf course, and I guarantee you there is *nothing* like you are describing *there*."

Perplexed, Marilyn dug around in her purse and found the letter she had earlier pulled from the envelope.

Looking at the letter, she said, "Oh, the letterhead at the top shows a *different* address than what's on the envelope." She then read off the address from the letterhead.

The stranger smiled, "*That's* where you want to go."

He then told us exactly how to get there.

The ladies and I looked at each other in stunned silence.

No one said a word as we pulled away, heading toward our destination. Molly finally broke the silence, "Where in the world did that man come from...and *how* did he know we were *lost...and why did he even care?*"

CHAPTER 29

Andy and Ambrose

Knoxville, Tennessee 1992

"Increasingly more of us, it seems, are becoming aware of the meaningful coincidences that occur every day. Some of these events are large and provocative. Others are small, almost imperceptible. But all of them give us evidence that we are not alone, that some mysterious spiritual process is influencing our lives."

—James Redfield

Raising money for something one can't see, hear, feel, or smell was just about as difficult as we had imagined. But Karen and I felt compelled to share our dream with others, whenever the opportunity arose. One day, while talking with a fellow clergy person, he told me that St. John's Cathedral Church in Knoxville had a large endowment, and that the trustees of the fund were always willing to consider worthy projects. That was all we needed to motivate us to make an appointment to talk with the Very Reverend James Sanders, Dean of the Cathedral.

On the way to Knoxville for our 10:30 a.m. appointment, we discussed what should be our approach to the Dean. Finally, we decided to simply tell him the story of our dream from the very beginning—the construction of a home for young men and women who are physically challenged, but who have normal cognitive function and need a place to live, a place where there were other young men and women like themselves, and caregivers who would assist them with things they were unable to do for themselves.

The dean was gracious and listened intently, as we introduced our vision and voiced hope that sufficient funds could be raised to begin the project. Our discussion seemed to be going well, when the dean glanced at his watch and said, "It's twelve o'clock. Could we continue our conversation over lunch? There's a good Italian restaurant not far from here."

The Italian decor of the restaurant and the aroma of the fine food made us feel like we had been set down in Naples or Milan. Seated, the three of us indulged in small talk, until we were interrupted by the waiter handing us menus and taking our drink orders. Some minutes later, we were fully engaged in conversation about the project, while simultaneously savoring the fare before us. Just as we were describing the various kinds of physical challenges the residents of the "Hosanna House" might have, I looked up and saw, coming into the restaurant, a young man who looked to be in his mid-twenties, pushing another young man in a wheelchair. I watched with increasing interest, as they were led by the greeter in our direction, over to the table *closest* to us, and then were seated *directly in front of the dean.* If the dean had not chosen this restaurant himself, I suspect he would have thought that the appearance of the two young men and their seating arrangement had been prearranged by *us.* I noticed the dean casting frequent glances over at the two young men, who appeared to be thoroughly enjoying each other's company, laughing and talking together, as the one helped in feeding the other.

When the dean got up to pay the bill, Karen and I stepped over to the two young men and introduced ourselves. They looked up with friendly smiles; then the one who was not in the wheelchair said, "I'm Andy, and this is Ambrose." We chatted briefly and left.

Four days later, on December 7, I noticed it was the feast day of *St. Ambrose of Milan,* and then it struck me that just seven days before, it had been the feast day of *St. Andrew.* "Hmmm...Andy and Ambrose," I reflected aloud.

"So wasn't it interesting," I said to Karen later, "meeting Ambrose and 'Andy,' *exactly halfway between their feast days.*"

Karen smiled, "Yeah, and here we were trying to help the dean visualize the kind of folks we were talking about...those who would form the Hosanna family...and here come these two guys. I mean, they materialized *right before his eyes.* All we needed by that time was a drum roll and a voice thundering, 'Exhibit A!'"

"Yeah, and don't you wonder what Ambrose thought about the 21st century Italian cuisine—you know, he *was* Bishop of Milan in the *fourth century.*"

CHAPTER 30

HAROLD

Maryland 1992

*"There is a Presence, an Intelligence, inspiring and guiding you;
there is a Power, a Law of Good, operating through that
Intelligence sustaining you."*

—Ernest Holmes

Debbi had just completed three years of college in a nursing program and was in the process of reassessing "her calling," which she earlier thought was to be a nurse. By the end of her third year of training, she finally realized this was really not her calling. Meanwhile, some friends told her about a group called "Walk Across America for Mother Earth." She decided to take at least a year out of academics and join them.

The group was organized in Belgium, and their plan was to meet on January 23rd at the United Nations building in New York, where they would begin their long walk across the country to the Nevada nuclear bomb test site (a.k.a., "NTS"). Their goal was to raise awareness of the dangers to the earth of nuclear proliferation.

It was a typical cold January morning in New York when approximately 140 walkers from Belgium, the United States, and several European countries met to begin their trek, first southward, toward Washington, then westward to their final destination. Standing with the crowd that morning outside the UN building, Debbi, who was born just a stone's throw north of the equator in Kenya, and who had spent most of her life in warm environments, shivered, as the final words of the send-off ceremony were delivered.

About two weeks into the walk, as they were approaching Washington, D.C., sludging through the slushy remains of a three-inch snow, Debbi began feeling the first pangs of a sore throat. Over the next several days she continued to get worse, until finally a full-fledged fever had set in, making the pack on her back feel like it had doubled in weight and her boots like lead. By then, she had fallen to the tail end of the group, and all that kept her going was the promise of a hot meal and a warm place to sleep in the basement of a Quaker Meeting House up ahead. She breathed a sigh of relief when she caught sight of the building, where she could see other hikers up ahead trudging into the welcoming light of the building.

As she dragged herself through the door, she could see that most of the other walkers had already arrived, and laid out their sleeping bags. While looking around for a spot to lay down her gear, a kindly-faced Quaker lady greeted her and pointed to a space where she could unload her pack.

"I'm Jeanne," she said, as she helped Debbi take off her pack. "You look like you need some food and something to drink," she added. "Come on downstairs and join us for dinner as soon as you're ready."

With a tray of steaming hot food in hand, Debbi began looking for a place to sit. Just then Jeanne reappeared. "May I sit with you? There's a spot over there," she said, leading Debbi over to a pair of empty seats.

Sipping on a cup of hot tea, Debbi looked over at Jeanne and said, "This warm tea feels so good on my throat."

"You look awfully tired," Jeanne observed. "In fact,

you look like you're coming down with something.

"I'm afraid I've already come down with whatever it is. I have a roaring sore throat and I feel hot."

Jeanne reached over and felt Debbi's forehead. "Wow, you really *are* hot! You definitely have a fever, and I think not just a little one."

"I'm not surprised," Debbi responded. "I've really been dragging the last several days."

The thought of Debbi sleeping with the others on the hard floor of the meeting room prompted Jeanne to say, "I'll tell you what, I have a guest room at my house where you could sleep much better. I'd like to take you home with me and put you to bed there. I'll keep you until you get over this thing. Then, when you feel up to it, I'll make sure you get back to your group. How's that?"

"That would be fantastic," Debbi agreed, exhaling a deep sigh of relief.

Resting comfortably in a guest room bed, Debbi barely moved during the next two days, while Jeanne periodically checked in on her and brought her food and drink. On the morning of the third day, Debbi was up on her feet and getting dressed, when she heard Jeanne bustling around in the kitchen. Walking in, she surprised Jeanne with a chipper "Good morning!"

"Hey, you're up!" Jeanne's face brightened. "You look a lot friskier this morning. I'm so glad."

"I feel a lot better now, thanks to you."

"Sit down and I'll fix you some breakfast," Jeanne said. "I'll bet you're hungry."

Debbi smiled...but instead of sitting down, she walked over to the refrigerator, where she noticed several pictures posted on its door. She looked at all the pictures, then, pointing to one, said, "Who is the man in this picture? He looks familiar."

"Oh that's my brother-in-law, Harold."

"Harold?" You know Harold? Harold Houghton...is your brother-in-law?"

Jeanne looked confused, then stared at Debbi in disbelief.

Debbi broke into a huge grin. "Yeah, I remember Harold very well. My first memory of him is when we lived in Nairobi and he used to come and have meals at our house. I was just five or six at the time, but I remember this blond guy named Harold, who used to come and visit us. My parents were the administrators of a program that sent young college graduates from the States to Kenya to teach in outlying schools. Harold taught in a small bush school in a remote part of Kenya, and he would come in periodically for R and R. Then, around ten years later, when we were living in Sewanee, he and his wife, Deborah, and their young boys visited us. I remember he mentioned how much he enjoyed staying with us in Nairobi, and especially the meals; because all he had to cook on out in the bush was a little one-burner stove." She paused, and then added, "I guess it's kinda' like I've been enjoying *your* home, and *your* home cooked meals right *here* for the past two days."

Jeanne was speechless, and just looked at Debbi, who by this time was smiling ear-to-ear. "I can't believe it!" Jeanne exclaimed. "Is this a *coincidence...or what!*"

CHAPTER 31

FLAT TIRE

Interstate 75 between Chattanooga and Greeneville, Tennessee
1999
"We are surrounded by a universal presence that responds to our
thoughts, words, and—especially—feelings."

—Eugene D. Holden

I was heading north on I-75, holding steady in my faithful little compact Mercury at seventy miles per hour, with a long way to go (160 miles) and not a lot of time to spare. The early service at St. James was at eight o'clock and I was the preacher. While not many people ever turned up for that early service, it *was* important to those who did, even on such a cold wintry morning.

Suddenly, I felt the rear end of the car beginning to weave. The moon had already set—which made everything dark as pitch—and I had a sinking feeling in my gut that I had just blown a tire. I slowed down and pulled over to the side of the freeway, hoping my instincts were wrong. Then I thought, *If my tire is flat, what can I do?* I had recently purchased this car, and I didn't even know where the equipment was to get the spare tire on.

Berating myself for not being better prepared, I turned on the car's interior light and made a fruitless search for a flashlight. When I opened the door to get out, the darkness hit me. I couldn't even see my hand in front of my face.

I felt my way around to the back of the car and stood motionless. Through the murky blackness, I could make out the vague outline of the vehicle. I could see a definite list to the right, confirming the fact that the right rear tire was flat.

I had no cell phone and no way to call for help. A feeling of unease washed over me, as I began to realize how alone I was in the middle of nowhere. The usually busy I-75 was nearly dead at this time on an early Sunday morning—every two minutes or so, a car or truck whizzed by.

Then, I had an idea. Aware that I was totally unable to help myself, I decided to do something I had never tried before. When I would see a vehicle coming, I would stand at the back of the car and wave vigorously, trying to flag down the car as it approached. I was hoping that my clerical collar might draw some sympathy and encourage a passer-by to stop and give a priest in trouble some help.

Standing at the rear of my car, breathing in the cold crisp air, I waited. Finally, a pair of headlights appeared in the distance. As it got closer, I began flailing my arms for all I was worth. When it sped by, I wondered if the driver had even seen me.

Soon, another pair of headlights appeared, but the car's driver zoomed by, just like the first, not even slowing down. I tried thinking what I must look like to someone speeding by. With my black coat blending with the darkness of the pre-dawn morning, probably all they could see was the white band of my clerical collar.

Then I had another idea. When the next car comes, I thought, I'll begin praying. Some words seemed to spontaneously form a prayer within me: "Dear God, ask the next driver to stop and help me, or to phone the highway patrol to come." While I believed in miracles, I added that second part of the prayer about the highway patrol, because it was beginning to dawn on me how crazy a person would have to be to stop under the cover of total darkness to try and help a stranger, a stranger who might just be dressed up as a priest.

When the next car appeared, I was still at the back of my car, waving and praying my heart out; but the car zoomed by without even slowing down. Because of the inky blackness, I couldn't see my watch. However, I knew that it would soon be so late that even if I *did* get help, there was no way I could make it to the church for the eight o'clock service.

Finally, in desperation, I had another idea. I would change just one word in my prayer. Instead of praying, "Dear God, *ask* the driver to stop," I would pray, "Dear God, *tell* the next driver to stop."

About one minute later, I saw another pair of headlights coming. When it was still some distance away, I began fervently praying my prayer, over and over, "Dear God, *tell* this driver to either stop and help me, or call the highway patrol to come." As it got closer, I could tell this one was big. The lights were bright and wide apart. When it was almost to me, I could see that it was an 18-wheeler. I kept praying, "Dear God, *tell* this driver..." Just as the huge truck was zooming past, there was a loud screeching of brakes! About fifty yards down the highway, the giant vehicle came to rest. I ran toward the truck and got to it, just as the driver was climbing down from the cab.

"Thank you, thank you, sir. Do you have a flashlight?" I could hardly believe it when he said he did not.

"I have some matches, though," he said, reaching into his coat pocket.

"I have a flat," I told him, "and it's so dark, I can't even find the equipment to get the car up and the tire off."

"Let's get the trunk open," he said, "and have a look." He lit a match and we rummaged around, until we found the lift, the lug wrench, and the spare.

Minutes passed, as we fumbled in the dim light of another three matches, trying to get the wheel cover off. Finally, he managed to loosen the wheel cover and it popped off. I felt a rush of hope, and told him, "I have an eight o'clock service in Greeneville."

His response was immediate and in monotone, "We'll get you there on time."

Finally, working together, we put on the spare and tightened the lug nuts. As he snapped the wheel cover back on, I thanked him again, and asked, "Do you have the time?"

His response, again, was a monotone, "We'll get you there on time."

I wasn't so sure. I knew it was getting late and I had a long way to go. With the job completed, I watched as he turned and walked away, disappearing into the darkness.

The first rays of light shown through a forest of trees, as I sped northward toward my destination. At the next town, I estimated how far I had to go and, checking my watch, it looked doubtful I could make it by eight. I pressed the gas pedal a little harder.

As I reached the outskirts of Greeneville, it was seven minutes before eight, and the church was in the center of town. I held my breath, trying not to hit any red lights.

Finally, with one block to go, I skidded around the corner and sped the last one-hundred-yard stretch, screeching into the church parking lot. I checked my watch. *It was exactly eight o'clock.*

Then the words of the trucker echoed in my mind: *"We'll get you there on time."*

CHAPTER 32

THERAPY DOG

Florence and Colorado Springs, Colorado 2011
"In service to God, we allow the Divine to touch, heal, soothe, bless
Its own through us."

—Diane Harmony

While heading home from shopping one evening, we pulled into the driveway of our good neighbor, Sandy Hodgson, to pick up some dishes we had taken there the day we celebrated the life of her late husband, Rocky, who had recently passed. But before we could even get out of the car, Karen's phone rang. It was Debbi.

"Where are you, Mama?"

"We're at Sandy's."

"You better get home as soon as you can. Something has happened to Ariel. She's hurting really, *really* bad."

We backed out of Sandy's driveway and headed up the bumpy, dirt road that winds its way up the mountain. Arriving home, we found our sweet blue merle Collie in a great deal of pain and unable to put any weight on her right hind leg. Karen immediately gave her enough pain medication to get her through the night.

X-rays the next morning showed that the ball of her right femur had pulled completely out of the socket. We had no idea how she could have done that, but Dr. Sadie was able to anesthetize her, pop the ball back into the socket, and put her in a sling. With this restriction in place, Ariel was unable to put any weight on that leg.

Four days later, the day before Thanksgiving, Ariel, still in her sling, once again showed signs of extreme pain, panting, shaking, and crying continuously. Another set of X-rays showed that the ball of her femur had *once again* pulled out of the socket.

"The only way to get it back in to stay is through surgery," Dr. Sadie told us. "If you like, I'll call the Canine Orthopedic Clinic in Colorado Springs to see if they would take you in. Being it's Thanksgiving Eve and already 3 o'clock, and it takes at least two hours to get there, well, I just hope the staff there will stay on to take care of her. I'll give them a call."

Two hours of Thanksgiving traffic later, we pulled into the orthopedic clinic in Colorado Springs. After more x-rays, the orthopedic surgeon, Dr. Swainson, came into the waiting room and explained the procedure he would be performing. While he was talking, his anesthetist, a young woman, came in to join him. She was already dressed out in her surgery smock and tight-fitting cap, and at a break in the conversation, she introduced herself. "I'm Cindy, and I'll be anesthetizing Ariel," she said with a sympathetic smile. "I understand you had a long drive to get here."

"Yes, we live about two hours south of here," I said.

"Where, exactly, do you live?" she asked.

"Up on the mountain between Florence and Wetmore."

"Really!" she said. "I have family in that area. My grandfather just passed away, but my grandmother is still there."

"What was your grandfather's name?" I asked. "I was an interim Hospice Chaplain in that area until just recently, so maybe I visited him."

"His name was Rocky Hodgson. He and my grandmother, Sandy..."

"Rocky! Rocky was your grandfather? He and Sandy were our neighbors, and I visited him just before he died at a nursing home in Canon City."

"Yes!" Karen said. "And Bekki and I took our therapy dogs to visit him there, as well. In fact, *this* therapy dog *right here*, who you are about to operate on, visited Rocky right before he died."

Cindy's eyes widened. "I'm not believing this."

Karen went on, "I remember how happy it made your grandfather just to see and pet Ariel, because he said he and your grandmother used to have blue merle Collies a long time ago."

I added, "While Ariel brought comfort to your grandfather, now, I guess it's *your time* to return the favor, and help bring some relief and comfort to *her*."

Cindy's eyes were moist, as were ours, as we all pondered the miracle of how, over the miles, we had all been brought together. Then she and Dr. Swainson left for the operating room, where Cindy gently placed her hands on Ariel, and put her to sleep for the operation.

Today, as I look out the window and watch Ariel happily romping and playing with the other dogs, it makes me think how we are *all* put here to take care of one another...and to bring comfort and joy to each other, *dogs and all.*

CONCLUSION

For as long as there has been recorded history, humans have experienced significant coincidental events. Lack of understanding of such experiences gave rise to the belief in spirits or a higher power that was beyond human control. Even in modern East Africa where I lived for ten years, the phrase, *Shari la Munguu*, meaning "Business of God," is commonly heard in reaction to unexplained, sometimes life-changing coincidences, such as when a man working in Nairobi, over 200 miles away from his home village, unexpectedly runs into a neighbor from home on a busy Nairobi street and the neighbor gives him the news that his child back home is very ill and he must immediately return to his village to care for his sick child.

During the past century scientists have made major breakthroughs relating to this "Business of God" that have left us awestruck with wonder. We are now told that mass and energy are interchangeable, and at the subatomic level, *all* is energy. *Everything.* What appears solid, like a table or a rock, is actually vibrating energy. We, ourselves, are a coalescence of energy, and part of the energetic life force that flows throughout the entire universe as a dynamic web of interconnection. Because of this interconnecting life force, our thoughts, feelings, and prayers, as well as our words and actions, can and do affect other people, as well as plants, animals, even ice crystals! It is as if our world of form is continually being woven into an exquisite, vibrant, ever-changing tapestry. Now and again we are privileged to catch a glimpse of the underside of the tapestry where the colorful threads intertwine. Perhaps in these moments, which we call "coincidences," we are simply being given a glimpse into another reality that has yet to be fully explored.

From early childhood we have been taught that we live in a cause-and-effect universe, one that behaves in *predictable* ways. But perhaps there is more—a deeper, yet-to-be-discovered order underpinning all of nature that is beyond our world of appearances and beyond our ability, at this time, to measure. When the person whom you accidentally bump into at the lunch counter shares an idea that completely turns your life around, your meeting may not have been "just a coincidence." Or when you go to work one day and find your desk and all your belongings have been moved out into the hall and then you go home and there is an invitation to your dream job waiting for you in the mail, it may not have been "just a coincidence."

As we continue to explore and become increasingly conscious of our interconnectedness with every other part of our living universe, we may be better able to understand *how* these wonder-filled moments occur. I believe science will continue to discover answers to the "how"question as we increasingly realize that the "supernatural" has been a part of our "natural" world all along, as Albert Einstein so wisely stated, "Either everything is a miracle or nothing is a miracle."

So the question remains—*why* do these things occur as they do?

I am reminded of the oft-repeated statement by Einstein: "The most important question a person can ask is, 'Is the universe a friendly place?' " A friendly universe is not a hostile universe that works against us; nor is it a neutral, I-don't-care universe; but rather, it is a universe that works with us and for us. It is a universe working behind the scenes, that you read about in the chapters of this book, that has convinced me, that in spite of the countless *unfriendly* forces at work in the world, causing wars and senseless chaos at every level, we live in a sea of Loving Energy, the same energy that created us, and continues to love us even when we totally mess up. This

Loving Energy that many of us call God reminds us, many times in the most incredibly synchronistic ways, that there is, indeed, a Power constantly manifesting in all creation, always conspiring for our ultimate good—my good, your good, and the good of every human being.

Yes, Professor Einstein, I believe the universe *is* a friendly place.

ACKNOWLEDGMENTS

With a grateful heart I salute and thank Dr. Jean
Reynolds, who saw something worth keeping in this story
and its message, and volunteered her editing and
publishing expertise to bring this book into being.

My heartfelt thanks go out to Diane Jones for her amazing
gift of layout and design.

I also honor and thank all the persons whose stories fill
the pages of this book due to our synchronistic
connections.

ABOUT THE AUTHOR

For the first 25 years of his life, the Reverend Dr. David Crippen did not realize the Universe was sending him messages. Then, an amazing synchronicity awakened him and changed his life forever. Could the Universe really be communicating with him?

He discovered that Carl Jung, a Swiss psychiatrist, had coined the term "synchronicity" to refer to an unexplained, meaningful coincidence, and that such an event can serve as guidance, affirmation, inspiration, or simply to remind us that God has a sense of humor.

David and his wife, Karen, began following the synchronicities until they became a guiding force in their lives; leading them and their young family to exotic lands, where David served as Curriculum Developer for the public schools in Kenya, Director of Refugee Relief and Development for Food for the Hungry International in Thailand, and Medical Director for refugee camps in Somalia for World Concern International.

As the synchronicities unfolded, David realized he was being led to enter the priesthood. Following ordination as an Episcopal priest, he established a group home for people with severe physical disabilities in Chattanooga, Tennessee and has served churches in Tennessee, Alabama, and Colorado for nearly 30 years.

Crippen's book for children, *Two Sides of the River*, has been widely used in schools throughout the U.S. as a tool to teach children how to make peace with those whom they perceive as their enemies.

He lives off the grid halfway up a mountain in Colorado with Karen; adult daughter, Bekki; three beloved Collies and Two Standard Poodles, all of whom are Certified Therapy Dogs; and a Norwegian Fjord Horse, Otis.

David holds five college and university degrees, but affirms that the synchronicities in his life have strengthened his faith far more than all his formal education. He believes that these unexplained, meaningful coincidences are one of God's primary ways of communicating with us—God's Beloved. They arrive in the lives of all of us, sometimes so complex and so astonishingly personalized that we know they could not have happened by chance. That, then, is the time to wake up, pay attention, and become aware that underneath the surface of our daily lives is another reality, a spiritual realm, where guidance is being offered to help us on our way.

Made in the USA
San Bernardino, CA
04 May 2017